9.75

BOOKS AND PERSONALITIES

BOOKS AND PERSONALITIES

By
H. W. NEVINSON

Essay Index Reprint Series

Essay Index

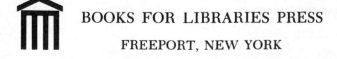

BOOKS FOR LIBRARIES PRESS

FREEPORT, NEW YORK

First published 1905
Reprinted 1968

LIBRARY OF CONGRESS CATALOG CARD NUMBER:
68-16962

INTRODUCTION

A S a general rule, I think, people like discussions upon subjects with which they are already well acquainted. A soldier who has been in a battle enjoys reading an account of it much more than the readers at home, though to him it is not news. The audience at a first night studies the dramatic critic's judgment next morning with far greater interest than the people who were not there—the people for whose information it was written. The man who has once slipped upon a cliff welcomes every story of mountaineering.

And so, in this collection of short studies in literature, I have included only such subjects as are quite familiar to every one who cares for literature at all. There is nothing abstruse or learned, nothing suited for specialists and professors, nothing outside the old road of those who pursue letters because they enjoy the pursuit. Every name is well known and of general interest. I think, also, that every name is regarded with admiration, and sometimes even with personal affection, by nearly all readers. For it is very seldom worth while to criticize bad or commonplace writers, just as there is little interest in scandal about nasty people.

Not long ago, there was a danger that the biographical side of literature would be overdone. The affairs of great poets like Shelley were treated with the exact solicitude due to lap-dogs or princes of the blood, and not to know the number of their children was taken as the mark of an unimaginative mind. Happily, we need now take very little account of all those disconnected items and details—the marriages, houses, and incomes—which seem so important to family relations. But we still care a great deal about the personality which lies behind all great literature, and may be discovered almost as completely in Homer and Shakespeare, of whose outward lives we know next to nothing, as in Johnson, Goethe, or Carlyle, whose lives we can follow year by year, and sometimes day by day.

And yet, though external things have little to do with personality, and the born humourist will be a humourist on a throne as well as in a ditch, I confess myself most attracted by writers whose personality has been exercised in big experience and varied fortune—men who have faced danger and degradation without losing their belief in the things that are out of danger and beyond degradation's reach. We may be certain that such writers are serious. There is something assured and quiet about their work, and they do not need to cry aloud. Even in criticism the same thing is partly true. The literary opinions of soldiers or bargemen are always worth hearing, when they have any at all. Sir Philip Sidney, being a soldier, was the man to write a defence of poetry, and I had rather listen to Ulysses talking upon Homer than read all the commentaries of German professors who have never sailed a ship. If a man's delight in literature has survived two or three campaigns or a visit to our colonies, it is likely to be genuine, and to have a book praised by one who has seen much and wandered far and been exposed to many kinds of death must, I think, be a great reward to the writer.

That is the kind of criticism which I have tried to follow—the broad and simple statement of the delight felt in certain books and certain writers by men who do not pursue literature as their business, but keep their love for it in the midst of other occupations and adventures. The self-denying studies of scholars and grammarians are universally admired. They are among the wonders of creation. But sometimes, in the intense interest which they arouse over phrases, words, and questions of interpretation, they make incautious people forget the delight and beauty of the soul for which literature exists. Then we demand that broader criticism which will renew our faith. For the service of criticism is to encourage the sense of beauty which some possess by nature, and to keep it alive by showing that others share it. Most of us, at all events, appreciate those excellences of literature best which we have partially discovered first for ourselves, and which have been afterwards pointed out to us by people whose character and opinions we admire.

The need and value of criticism have often been doubted; but I do not doubt them now. The innate sense of beauty will sometimes go right of itself, just as a boy from a Workhouse School sometimes becomes a fine character. But far more often it goes astray for want of guidance, and wastes itself on follies, or else, pining for sympathy's nourishment, it dies. We need not count ourselves among those who would restrain reading within the rigid lines of " the best." We know how large is the quantity of the best, and how fast we are all running towards death, leaving the greater part even of the best unknown. But still, in reading, as in life, we would have a man a little reckless and not too careful of his fate. No one's life or reading matters so much as all that, or if it does, it is a pity a man should think so, for then he may lose the object of life and reading too. And yet, even in the utmost recklessness of literary adventure or debauch, the lover of literature who has once felt the power of true criticism will never be in doubt as to his surroundings, and when he returns to the best it will be with the sense of security and joyful expectation that a happy warrior feels in going home.

Many of the following studies and reviews have appeared already in the *North American Review*, the *Speaker*, the *Academy*, the *Book Monthly*, and the *Daily Chronicle*, and they are here collected and re-issued with due acknowledgment.

H. W. N.

CONTENTS

	PAGE
INTRODUCTION	V
HEINRICH HEINE	I
GOETHE'S BIRTHDAY, AUGUST 28, 1899	35
"SWEETNESS AND LIGHT"	41
(MATTHEW ARNOLD'S NOTE-BOOKS.)	
THE PHILOSOPHIC MIND	49
(EPICTETUS.)	
THE LAST OF THE PROPHETS	57
(MR. FREDERIC HARRISON'S "RUSKIN.")	
THE LAST OF ROMANCES	66
("THE SUNDERING FLOOD," BY WILLIAM MORRIS.)	
WEDDED GENIUS	73
("NEW LETTERS AND MEMORIALS OF JANE WELSH CARLYLE.")	
"FORBEARE!"	83
("THE NEMESIS OF FROUDE.")	
"CARLYLE'S LETTERS"	90
("NEW LETTERS OF THOMAS CARLYLE.")	
THE POET LOVERS	99
("LOVE LETTERS OF ROBERT BROWNING AND ELIZABETH BARRETT BARRETT.")	

xi

PAGE

THE POET OF GROTESQUE 116
(MR. CHESTERTON'S "BROWNING.")

THE MASTER OF COMEDY 123
(MR. ROGERS'S "ARISTOPHANES.")

ÆSCHYLUS AT STRATFORD, 1904 129

THE "ALCESTIS" AT BRADFIELD 136

DRAMAS IN WHISPER 142
(MÆTERLINCK'S PLAYS.)

FROM LEITH TO SAMOA 149
(MR. GRAHAM BALFOUR'S "LIFE OF STEVENSON.")

MEREDITH 162

THOMAS HARDY 169

THE LILLIPUT WORLD 173
(MR. HARDY'S "DYNASTS.")

BEARDSLEY 179

THE GENTLE CRAFT 188
(IZAAK WALTON'S "COMPLEAT ANGLER.")

A MEMORIAL TO SIR THOMAS BROWNE 191

IF I WERE FITZGERALD ! 196
(MR. LE GALLIENNE'S "RUBÁIYÁT.")

AN OMARIAN SERVICE 204
(MR. HERON-ALLEN'S "RUBÁIYÁT.")

OMAR AGAIN 213
(PROFESSOR YORK POWELL'S "QUATRAINS FROM OMAR.")

THE POET OF THE SIDHE 218
(MR. WILLIAM YEATS'S "POEMS.")

Contents

PAGE

THE LATTER OISIN 226
("THE SHADOWY WATERS," BY MR. W. B. YEATS.)

"A. E." 233
(MR. GEORGE RUSSELL'S POEMS.)

BATTLES LONG AGO 239
(LADY GREGORY'S "GODS AND FIGHTING MEN.")

IRISH PLAYS OF 1904 245

"THE DARK ROSALEEN" 251

PAST AND PRESENT 268
(JOCELIN'S CHRONICLE.)

THE WHITE ROSE 277
(MR. ANDREW LANG'S "PRINCE CHARLES EDWARD.")

DE WET 286
("THREE YEARS' WAR.")

A PRIEST OF SLUMS 295
("LIFE OF FATHER DOLLING.")

EXUBERANCE 303
(MR. HILAIRE BELLOC'S "CALIBAN'S GUIDE TO LETTERS.")

THE FAITH OF LITERATURE 311

BOOKS AND PERSONALITIES

Heinrich Heine

" But was it thou—I think
Surely it was—that bard
Unnamed, who, as Goethe said,
Had every other gift, but wanted love ;
Love without which the tongue
Even of angels sounds amiss ? "

THESE prosaic lines of Matthew Arnold are the badge which probably most Englishmen attach to Heine. And in answer to the question which they ask, we can only say, " No, it was not. Heine was not that bard." Never would Goethe have said such a thing. And as a matter of fact that bard unnamed has been named any time these thirty years, and the name we read is not Heine's, but Heine's bitterest enemy's—a man whom Heine literally put to death by his scorn.[1] It was of Platen, a mere aristocrat, a

---

[1] "Eckermann's Conversations," December 25, 1825 : "Then we spoke of Platen, whose negative tendency was also (as well as Byron's) disapproved. 'There is no denying his many brilliant qualities,' said Goethe, 'only he lacks Love. He loves his readers and his fellow poets as little as himself, and so we can apply to him the saying of the

languid amateur, a half-hearted hedonist, a man whom Heine publicly accused of all the unnatural crimes not even mentioned in the Decalogue—it was of Count Platen that Goethe used the famous words. Yet even in Germany they were applied to Heine for half a century, and they stick to him still. Such irony of fate is but what might be expected. It was God's last touch to the ironic poem which he wrote in the flesh and blood of Heine's life—a poem in Heine's own best manner.

The Almighty began the opening lines of this little lyric of a life with unerring skill. Time and place were excellently chosen. "Over my cradle," Heine said, " the last moonbeams of the eighteenth century and the earliest sunlight of the nineteenth met together." He was born in the last month of the eighteenth century. At the very start we find that division of nature which runs through all his character and work. We are caught in the moon-beams of dreamy olden ways, the moonbeams of yearning and tender love, of deep forests where nightingales sing, and of fields where the smell of hidden violets suddenly takes the belated traveller back to the mystery of youth. Then the sun of the nineteenth century rises with all the joy of morning, with the clearness and sanity of the day, the laughter

Apostle, "Though I speak with the tongue of men and angels and have not Love," etc. I have been reading Platen's poems lately. Yes, he has talent ; but he is without Love, and so he will never work as he ought to have done.' "

of warmth and work. Men and women go about their labour, and the railway train whistles. All is bright and definite. But there is perhaps just a touch of disillusion, of cruelty in all the vivid reality and exactitude.

In race and place the poet's destiny was equally characteristic. He was a Jew and a German, and in his childhood his birthplace on the Rhine suddenly became subject to France. As a Jew he was bound by ritual and symbolism to an almost prehistoric past. He was brought up to revere the most ancient by far of all surviving gods. In his heart were mingled the humiliation and pride of the downtrodden, crafty, God-elected race—that thieving dog of Judah (it is his own comparison) which is kicked about the streets all week, but on the sabbath is released as from an evil enchantment and becomes a king again. As a German he was heir to a wealth of dreams and grandmotherly tales, to a wide, if watery, culture, to Germany's tender, babbling language, and her tender, tearful old heart. And into his young life came France, like sunlight indeed —the irresistible France of the Revolution and the early Empire, the goddess of freedom with the young rays of sanity and reason still blazing on her forehead. Every one knows Heine's saying that the Englishman loves liberty as his wedded wife ; the Frenchman loves her as his mistress ; the German as his grandmother. Well, Heine loved Judaism as a divorced

wife, whose charms in half-wakeful hours he sometimes recalled with regret. Germany he loved as
his grandmother—no, as his mother, to whose side
he could always return for consolation like a solitary
child. But France was a mistress to him—to him
as to others.

His youth and early manhood were passed in a
time of singular stagnation both in politics and
literature. It was the time of the Holy Alliance—
the reaction towards tyranny which set in after
Waterloo, and held all Europe enchained for fifteen
years. Kings and Governments again ventured to
put on airs of importance, and became a public
nuisance. In letters, Goethe was nominally supreme,
but his real service was over, and he was old and
decorated. The main force in German literature
was the Romantic School, but each year it was
becoming more absurd in its endeavour to restore
the mystical beauty of the Middle Ages by an
affected and patchwork faith, which twenty years
ago we might have called a Grosvenor-Gallery
Christianity. The school had taken its place in the
Holy Alliance, and was the agent of despotism.
Heavy patriots boasted of it as the ornament of that
sluggish Germanity which is always so ready to wrap
itself in the bear-skin of its own manners and roar
defiance across the Rhine : just as England sometimes wraps herself in the wet blanket of her own
virtue. It was a dull and motionless time. " You

would think," said Heine, "that there was nobody
in Germany but monthly nurses and dramatic
critics."

In the midst of these domestic interests Heine's
youthful works suddenly appeared. They consisted
of some records of student tours and some chapters
of early reminiscence, in a whimsical but brilliant
prose, something after Sterne's manner. And, besides, there were three short series of lyrics, collected
in 1827 under the famous title of "A Book of
Songs." In the scenes of memory and travel is
revealed the figure of a young student wandering
through the forests in freedom, crossing the mountains into Italy, full of the capacity for joy, setting
at nought all the established traditions of European
life, worshipping light and liberty and France with
equal conviction, deriding Germany's most cherished
ideals, and choosing Napoleon as his mythical hero,
deified already.

"What were my feelings," he cries, "when I saw him
once with my very own eyes—him, the Emperor?
Hosannah in the Highest!

"He was in the avenue of the Court gardens at Düssel-
dorf. As I pushed through the gaping crowd, I thought of
the deeds and battles which M. Le Grand had played me
on his drum ; my heart beat the Imperial March, and yet I
could not help remembering the order of police ordaining a
penalty of fifteen shillings for any one found riding along
the avenue. And the Emperor and his suite rode along the
avenue, the trees trembled and bowed before him as he

went, the sun's rays peered with quivering curiosity through the green foliage, and in the blue heaven above him hung a golden star in all men's sight. The Emperor was wearing his unpretentious green uniform, and the little cocked hat famous round the world. He rode a white horse, which trod the earth so proudly, so calmly, with such distinction—had I been Crown Prince of Prussia I should have envied that horse. The Emperor sat carelessly, loosely almost ; one hand held the rein, the other good-naturedly patted the horse's neck. It was a gleaming hand, like marble, a powerful hand, one of the two hands which had chained the many-headed monster of confusion and guided the battles of the world—and it patted the horse's neck good-naturedly. The face, too, was the colour of some Greek or Roman bust in marble, the features were chiselled on the same noble lines as the antique, and on the face stood written, ' Thou shalt have none other gods but me.' A smile which warmed and cheered all hearts hovered over the lips—and yet we knew those lips had only to whistle and Prussia was wiped out of existence—those lips had only to whistle and the death-bell sounded for the whole clerical party—those lips had only to whistle, and all the Holy Roman Empire would be set dancing. And those lips smiled, and the eye smiled too. It was an eye clear as the heavens. It could read the hearts of men. It saw at one glance all things in this world together, whilst others saw them in succession or as coloured shades. The forehead was not so clear ; spirits of future battles were lurking there, and sometimes a ripple passed over the brows ; it was the creative thoughts, the great seven-leagued boots of thought, with which the Emperor's soul strode invisible over the world, and I think each of those thoughts would have given a German author plenty of material to write about for the rest of his life.

"The Emperor is dead. . . . Strange ! His three greatest

opponents have already been overtaken by a terrible fate. Londonderry has cut his throat, Louis XVIII. has rotted on his throne, and Professor Saalfeld is still a professor in Göttingen."

From the first the peculiar beauty of Heine's songs has puzzled and eluded the critics, just as the beauty of a rose eludes the botanist, or a woman's beauty eludes the *post mortem*. Among the earliest German criticisms I find an explanation which is as good as any other—

" Mr. Heine is at one and the same time beautifully objective and yet so marvellously subjective ; or perhaps we might express the secret of his art still more clearly by calling him marvellously objective in his beautiful subjectivity."

No doubt for this reason his poems attracted immediate attention. By the age of thirty he was famous—that is to say, he was hated, maligned, envied, denounced, reviled, and loved as perhaps no other poet of recent years has been, except Byron. Within his lifetime the " Book of Songs " had an enormous sale. He used to say that if he wanted to see a monument to his popularity in Germany, he would stand and contemplate the beautiful mansion which his publisher had built for himself at Hamburg. It is a glorious moment in the life of a poet or any writer when wealth and success at last crown his publisher.

For the form of his verse Heine almost always

chose the very simplest of all metres, the four-line
stanza of the old ballad and Volkslied—full of tender
associations, going to the heart of the people.   With
patient and remorseless care he pruned and simplified
this verse into an instrument exactly suited to his
purpose, and the surprise of finding a feeling so
profound and so modern an irony in such a childlike
and ancient form is one of his special charms.   The
Romantic poets and Goethe himself had used similar
metres.   With the Romantic poets Heine always
had much sympathy, though he destroyed their
influence.   He always thought of himself as the last
of their number—"a Romanticist unfrocked," as a
French critic called him.   But for substance he
refused to be put off with their theatrical encum-
brances.   He refused also to imitate the so-called
Nature-poets in their easy-going rhymes on the
beauties of creation, and the gratitude due to God,
following the common prescription for a German
song—take Sonne and Wonne, add Schmerz and
Herz, and stir up with a little Wehmuth.   At the
bottom of his wildest and sweetest dreams, his
nightingale songs, his haunted moonlight, his Indian
visions, there lurks the modern thought, the heart
and brain of Heine himself, a man of the nineteenth
century, quite alive to the time of day.   "It is fairly
easy," he writes, "to recognize the poetry of the
past.   But only a great poet can perceive the poetry
of his own times."

Englishmen demand two qualities chiefly from a lyric poet—the two qualities of reality and brevity. And if that is so, Heine should be especially dear to us. The poems of his maturity are always of present interest and unmistakable meaning. In all his works I only know one where the intention is not perfectly clear ("Nächtliche Fahrt"). And as to brevity, the average length of his songs is not more than twelve or sixteen short lines ; many of the best only run to eight ; some to four.

This excellent gift of brevity and the self-restraint which relies so much on the understanding of the reader is at the root of a peculiar quality most characteristic of Heine, but hard to fix and define. I have heard it called lyrical irony. It is a sudden reserve at the very moment when emotion is at its height, a refusal to do more than hint at the depth of feeling in the poet's mind. It comes quickly, generally at the end of a poem, sometimes almost with a shock, and it is a sure defence against sentimentality and the boredom which a long rhapsody of personal and intimate feelings almost always produces. In English it may be illustrated by a few familiar examples, all in Heine's spirit—

> "With lightsome heart I pu'd a rose
> Frae off its thorny tree ;
> And my fause lover staw the rose,
> And left the thorn wi' me."

Or—

> "She lived unknown, and few could know
>   When Lucy ceased to be ;
> But she is in her grave, and O !
>   The difference to me."

Or—

> " Yet I will but say what mere friends say,
>   Or only a thought stronger ;
> I will hold your hand but as long as all may,
>   Or so very little longer ! "

And from Heine take as instances—

> " Out of my great sorrows
> I make my little songs :
> They lift their rustling wings
> And flutter to her heart.
> They find their way to my beloved,
> But they come to me again and lament,
> And lament, and will not tell me
> What they saw in her heart."

Or—

> " When two part from one another
> They give their hands,
> And begin to weep
> And sigh without end.
> We did not weep,
> We did not sigh 'Woe !' and 'Alas !'
> The tears and sighs—
> They came afterwards."

Or—

> " Death—that is the cool night,
> Life is the sultry day ;
> It is growing dark now, and I am falling asleep,
> The day has made me weary.

Over my bed stands a tall tree,
A young nightingale is singing on it;
She sings of love, love, love,
I hear it in my dreams."

Or—

" Our hearts have concluded
    The Holy Alliance ;
They came close to one another,
    And there was no misunderstandings.
Ah, but the tender roses
    Which lay upon your bosom,
Poor little witnesses to the treaty,
    They were almost crushed to death."

Or—

" The letter you wrote
    Gives me no pain,
It is true you will love me no more,
    But your letter is long.
Twelve sides, so close and neat,
    Quite a little manuscript !
One does not write at such exhaustive length
    When one ordains a final parting."

Or—

" Have no fear, beloved heart,
    You are safe here as safe can be :
Have no fear : to keep out robbers,
    See, I draw the bolt.

" No matter how the wind may rage,
    There is no danger for the house ;
To prevent any fear of fire,
    See, I put out the lamp.

"Oh, permit me to entwine
    My arm about your neck :
One catches cold so easily
    For want of a shawl."

And compare the later poems—

JENNY.

" I am now thirty-five years old,
    And you are hardly fifteen—
O Jenny, when I look at you
    The ancient dream awakes again.

" In the year eighteen hundred and seventeen
    I saw a girl wonderfully like you
In form and nature.
    She wore her hair too just the same.

" ' I'm going to the university,'
    I said to her.   ' I am coming back
In but a little time ; wait for me.'
    She answered, ' You are my only joy.'

" For three years I had studied the Pandects,
    When on the first of May
In Göttingen I heard the news
    That my beloved was married.

" It was on the first of May.   The spring
    Marched laughing and green through field and dell,
The birds sang, and every worm
    Rejoiced in the sunshine.

" But I turned pale and sick,
  And all my powers left me :
God alone can know
  What I suffered at night.

" But I got well. My health
  Is now as strong as an oak—
O Jenny, when I look at you
  The ancient dream awakes again."

Or—

" At the dawn of a summer morning
  I go about the garden.
The flowers whisper and speak,
  But I wander in silence.
The flowers whisper and speak,
  And look at me with sympathy :
They say, ' Be not angry with our sister,
  You pale and mournful man.' "

Or—

" When once you are my married wife,
  You will be a very enviable woman,
You will live in nothing but a round of delight,
  In nothing but pleasure and joy.

" And if you scold and if you rage,
  I'll bear it patiently ;
Only, if you don't praise my verses,
  I will obtain a judicial separation."

Or—

" There was an old, old king,
  His heart was heavy, his head was grey ;
The poor old king
  He took to himself a young wife.

" There was a pretty page,
Yellow was his head, light was his heart :
He carried the silken train
For the young queen.

" Do you know the old song ?
It sounds so sweet, it sounds so sad !
Both of them had to die,
They loved each other far too well."

But this so-called Lyrical Irony, with its fine reserve of emotion, is only one phase of Heine's irony. He has irony of other kinds—the assumed ignorance, the affected simplicity, and the kind which is so often confounded with cynicism. It has always been the common charge of gentle readers, especially of German readers, that Heine is " so cynical." They say he does not leave one with that sense of restful satisfaction which is so popular with readers that publishers are tempted to esteem it the object of all literature. Well, it is hard to be perfect, but if I were a poet I should rather be called cynical than maudlin. And if I wanted other help than words, I would go to a cynic rather than to a sentimentalist. And there are distinctions in cynicism. There is the vulgar cynicism of the clubs, of the common comfortable man—and there is the cynicism, springing from the contrast between the visions of the mind and the ugliness, horror, and tedium of average human reality. That may be called the cynicism of a Quixote disillusioned. But the quixotic temperament can never be stifled. Under the hardened and chilly surface it smoulders still, ever ready to kindle into flame at the breath of some noble and uncalculating passion. This kind of cynicism was Heine's, and what Heine said of Sterne may be said of himself—

" Sterne, like Shakespeare, was brought up by the Muses on Parnassus. But as women will, they ruined him too soon, chiefly by their caresses. He was the bosom-child of the pale goddess of Tragedy. Once in a paroxysm of cruel tenderness she kissed his young heart so hard, with such power of love, putting her whole soul into the touch, that the heart began to bleed, and suddenly understood all the sorrows of this world, and was filled with endless pity. But the younger daughter of Memory, the rosy goddess of Mirth, sprang to his side, and took the suffering child into her arms, and sought to cheer him with laughter and song, and gave him as a plaything her comic mask and bells, and kissed him gently on the lips, and kissed into him all her merriment, all her defiant joy, all her mocking wit."

The peculiar melancholy of Heine has received the name of World Sorrow. It is a mood that belongs to negative periods, to a time of reaction after high hopes and inspiring effort. It comes to men and to nations in those dull lengths of days when they add up the gains of all their endeavours and see how small is their sum. The struggle seems to have availed nothing, and things seem to remain as they have been. For want of action, for want of the healthy stir of combat, the mind turns in upon itself.   The Philistines, then, will triumph for ever. They still possess the promised land.   They are perhaps right after all in taking comfort from the good things of this life, in maintaining their complacent, church-going indifference to the long and irremediable woe.   As often happens, Heine's world-sorrow was coloured all the blacker by his own private sorrow—his uncertainty of life and aim, his self-disgust at having submitted to Christian baptism, and the pangs of despised love.   The expression of it gave a fine shock to easy satisfaction.   And in a man so full of inward happiness, so framed for joy and Greek blitheness of life, it forms one of those sharp contrasts of which Heine is made up.   It comes upon us in the sudden turns of many poems, and is the theme of " The Twilight of the Gods."

" The May has come with its golden lights and silken breezes and the smell of spices, and in joyful wise she entices us with her white blossoms, and greets us from a thousand blue violet eyes, and spreads a carpet of flowering green, interwoven with sunshine and morning dew, and calls the dear children of men to see it all.   The simple people obey her first summons ; the men put on their nankeen trousers and the Sunday coat with yellow shining buttons ; the women clothe themselves in the white of innocence ; young men stroke their spring moustaches ; girls let their bosoms swell ; the town poets stick paper and pencil and glasses in their pockets—and with joy the varied crowd tramps to the gates, and encamps upon the green turf outside, marvels to see the trees so busy growing, plays with the bright and dainty flowers, listens to the song of merry birds, and shouts with joy to the high vault of heaven.

"To me the May came too. She knocked three times at my door, and cried, 'I am the May ; pale dreamer, come I will kiss thee.' I kept my door fast bolted, and cried, 'In vain enticest thou me, thou evil guest. I have looked thee through and through ; I have looked through the structure of the world, and have seen too much, and far too deep, and all joy is departed, and endless torments have entered into my heart. I see through the hard and stony rinds of men's houses and men's hearts, and see in both lies and deceit and misery. On their faces I read their thoughts, and evil are they all. In the maiden's blush of shame I see a hidden desire trembling ; on the proudly inspired head of youth I see the gay and mocking cap and bells ; and only apish masks and sickly shadows do I see upon this earth, and I know not whether it be a madhouse or a hospital. I look into the depths of old earth, as though it were of crystal, and I see the horror which May strives in vain to cover with her joyful green. I see the dead : they lie down there in narrow coffins, their hands folded and their eyes open, white is their shroud and white their countenance, and through their lips the yellow worms are crawling. I see the son sitting with his mistress for pastime upon his father's grave ; nightingales sing mocking songs around, the tender meadow-blossoms smile maliciously, the dead father raises himself in his grave, and old mother earth shudders with pain.

"Thou, poor earth, I know thy sorrows. I see the fire that boils within thy bosom, and I see thy thousand veins bleeding, and how thy wounds are torn gaping wide, and flame and smoke and blood stream wildly out. I see thy insolent, gigantic sons, primeval brood, rise from the black abysses, brandishing red torches in their hands. They set

c

their iron ladders to, and storm wildly up into the feast or heaven ; and black dwarfs climb after them, and all the golden stars above pass crackling away. With impious hand they tear the golden curtain from God's own tent ; howling, the pious hosts of angels fall down upon their faces. On His throne God sits, and He turns pale ; He tears the crown from His head and rends His hair; and nearer and nearer the wild rout presses on. The giants hurl their red torches into the wide kingdom of heaven, the dwarfs beat the angels' backs with scourges of flame—the angels twist and writhe in torment, and are hauled away by the hair. And there I see my own dear angel with her fair locks and face so sweet, with the eternal love about her mouth, and the joy of heaven in her blue eyes ; and a hatefully ugly black kobold tears her from the ground—my pale white angel—grins as he eyes her lovely limbs, embraces her fast with lustful embrace—and a shrill cry goes shrieking through the universe, the columns break, earth and heaven fall together, and primeval night takes up her reign."

In the midst of his world-sorrow—his increasing gloom and self-despair, his oppression at the dreary outlook of all that made for progress—Heine, like the rest of Europe, was roused by the Three Days or July—the Revolution of 1830. The sun of freedom had again risen, and again in France. All who loved the light welcomed it with the insanity of released prisoners. It was in any case becoming impossible for Heine to remain longer in Germany. In all Prussia his works were forbidden. He himself was already an exile, subject to long imprisonment if he crossed the frontier. In autumn he set off for Paris,

and but for two brief visits to Hamburg fourteen
years later, he never quitted France again. It is
true that when his fatal illness was crawling upon
him, he sent a petition through Alexander von
Humboldt to the King of Prussia asking to be
allowed to come to Berlin to consult a famous
physician, an old school friend, to whom he trusted
for alleviation of his agony. But the petition was
naturally refused, without phrase. What is the
good of being a king if you may not slaughter your
subjects as you please ?

But Heine was only thirty when he crossed the
Rhine for good—crossed, as he said, the Jordan
which separates the children of light from the land
of the Philistines. The next ten years were the
happiest of his life. In these first years in Paris,
life with its brilliancy and intoxication did indeed
appear to him " like the dream of a drunken god."
He was welcomed into a circle of genius. Balzac,
Victor Hugo, Berenger, George Sand, Alfred de
Musset, Gautier, Berlioz, Liszt, were only some of
the leading names. Into this band Heine threw
himself like a zealot of a new religion. To him for
the time this new life was a new religion ; and as is
said in one of the most beautiful of his early poems,
he did indeed regard himself as a knight of the
Holy Spirit.

" Now that I am grown up and have read much and
travelled far, my heart is wider, and with all my heart I

believe in the Holy Spirit. It was He who worked the
greatest miracles, and He is working greater still. He
broke the castles of tyrants and the yoke of the slave. He
heals up the deadly wounds and renews the justice of old.
All men are born to equal rights, and in His eyes they are
all a race of nobles. He scares away the evil mists and
ghosts of the brain, which mar our love and pleasure, and
grin at us by night and day. The Holy Spirit has elected a
thousand knights, well armed, to fulfil His word, and has
breathed His courage upon them. Their dear swords flash,
their fine banners wave! Ah, my sweet child, would you
like to behold these knights so proud? Look on me, sweet
child. Kiss me, and look me straight in the eyes; for I
myself am one of the Holy Spirit's knights."

And this new religion was not entirely a dis-
embodied ghost of a thing. As a student in Berlin
Heine had been rather intimate with Hegel. He
had laughed at him, it is true—

" Too fragmentary is this world and life !
  I must betake myself to the German professor,
  Who well knows how to fit life together
  And make a comprehensible system out of it :
  With his night-caps and patches of old dressing-gowns
  He stops up the holes in the construction of the universe."

Yet he was much under Hegel's influence.
Without caring a jot about metaphysics, he welcomed
Hegel's popular results—that Being and Knowing
are identical, that all existence is full of reason, that
the ideal world is nothing else than the real, that the

highest aim of the human spirit is " Das Zu-sich-selbst-kommen " (Oh, what a language !).

" It flattered my vanity," he wrote afterwards, " to be told that God was not, as my grandmother supposed, the dear God who resided in heaven, but that I myself on this earth was the dear God. . . . I was the primeval morality, I was incapable of sin. I was purity incarnate. . . . I had no enemy left, but only unbelievers who had doubts as to my Godhead."

To the young nothing could be more inspiring than this kind of Pantheism. A believer in it will certainly be likely to surpass the level Christian in virtue and self-sacrifice ; for if *noblesse oblige*, it surely follows that Godhead has stronger obligations still. And in Paris Heine found an actual church in which similar doctrines were proclaimed. Independently of Hegel, the followers of St. Simon had arrived at like conclusions on the inherent Godhead in man, though their tenets were rather social than meta-physical. They were now trying to establish a European League of Labour, under which each was to receive what he had gained by his actual work, and " the exploitation of man by man " was for ever to cease. Another attractive doctrine was " the rehabilitation of the flesh "—the restoration of the body to an equal place with the spirit ; for if the whole man was divine, the old distinction of body and soul vanished. This new religion had set up a church with a ritual and a high-priest, and

many came to pray, and some remained to scoff.
Carlyle, as we know, was at this time much drawn
by its doctrine, and but for Goethe's prudent
warning, gods and men might perhaps have beheld
Carlyle and Heine worshipping side by side in the
same pew, and holding the same hymn-book between
them, like lovers in a chapel. But unhappily the
new religion went to pieces soon afterwards on the
woman question. Was woman as well as man
entitled to the full rights and liberties of incarnate
deity ? Was the tree of knowledge—the tree of
liberty—equally wholesome for her ? Alas ! whilst
men were arguing in the new Church, woman took
the question into her own sweet hands, as in the
old Paradise, and for a second time she was responsible for the Fall. The Church collapsed. Many
of the gods sought to solve the question by marriage,
trying if it were possible for male and female divinities
to live on decent terms under the same roof. The
high-priest Enfantin set off to Egypt on a commission
to control the Nile by a system of dams, and, though
he failed, he found that ancient river much more
submissive to his divine will than were the incarnate
ladies of Paris.

For the time Heine welcomed St. Simonism
because it fell in with his sanguine theory. Yet by a
characteristic contradiction he kept for the old Deism
of his fathers, as for all the moonlit memories of
childhood, a childlike tenderness, and in the passages

of his utmost irony, he still handles his God as though he loved him. With what tenderness he approaches his account of the destruction of Deism under Kant's remorseless critique !

"Next time we will speak of this catastrophe—this 21st January of Deism. A peculiar awe, a mysterious piety, prevents me from writing more to-day. My heart is full of a terrible pity—it is old Jehovah himself who is making ready for death. We have known him so well from his cradle up, in Egypt, where he was nurtured among divine calves, crocodiles, sacred onions, ibises, and cats. We have seen how he bade adieu to these playmates of his childhood, and the obelisks and sphinxes of his native Nile, and how he became a little god-king in Palestine among a poor shepherd tribe, and lived in his very own temple-palace. We saw later how he came into contact with the Assyrian-Babylonian civilization, and laid aside his all-too-human passions, no longer spitting out rage and vengeance—at all events, no longer visiting every human folly with his thunder. We saw him emigrate to Rome, where he renounced all national prejudices, proclaimed the equality of all races in the eyes of heaven, and set up an opposition to old Jupiter with such beautiful phrases and prolonged intrigues that he obtained dominion over him, and from the Capitol ruled the city and the world. We saw how he became more and more spiritualized, how he uttered the lamentations of a gentle saint, how he became a loving father, a universal friend of man, a benefactor to the human race, a philanthropist indeed —but it all availed him nothing in the end.

"Do you hear the tinkling of a little bell ? Fall on your knees ! They are bearing the sacraments to a dying God."

One attraction of the New Pantheism, this spiritualization of matter, this rehabilitation of the flesh, was, in Heine's case, the stimulus which it gave to pleasure. It cast a kind of sanctification over the bodily pleasures, and to these Heine was as keenly alive as most of us are. The charm of French cookery, the charm of French women—these were things that for a long time made exile seem a translation into a heaven of a kind. "This dish," he once said in a restaurant, "should be eaten on our knees." And in honour of the French women whom he loved, he wrote that series of poems which gave such scandal to his enemies in Germany, and which are so full of the tenderness, the irony, the very essence of untrammelled affections. In his book on Ludwig Börne there is a true passage on this subject. He had been complaining of some German writer who had asserted there was not a woman on the streets of Paris whose charms were unknown to Heine.

"I can assure the author," he continues, "that even in my wildest youth I have not known a woman unless I was inspired by her beauty—that incarnate revelation of God— or by the true passion, that true passion which is also of divine origin, because it liberates us from all mean and selfish emotions, and drives us to sacrifice all the empty blessings of life, and even life itself for the beloved. And the world in the end is just, and pardons the flame, if only the fire is strong and genuine, throws a fine light, and lasts long. The world is hard upon a brief and empty fire of straw, and mocks at all cautious and half-hearted warmth. But it respects and honours passion when once it has proved itself to be genuine ; and in that case time brings with it a certain legitimacy."

Well, constancy was certainly not one of Heine's own attributes ; but after he had been four years in Paris, he entered into a fairly stable agreement with a very beautiful, uneducated Belgian shop-girl, whom he bought from her mistress for £120. Six years later he married her legally, fearing that by some unforeseen accident he might be killed in a French duel to which his writings had driven him. They lived together till the end. She was a steady-going Catholic, subject to violent fits of fury ; she never learnt enough German to read a line of Heine's poems, and, in fact, could hardly read at all ; she tormented him by an insane passion for petty cleanliness, and lavished all the wealth of a woman's affection upon her cockatoo. Heine was certainly not more unhappy with her than most men of genius have been with their wives—not nearly so unhappy as the wives have been with most men of genius. He protected her very tenderly ; but in dress and food she was magnificently extravagant, and they were almost continually in debt. His millionaire uncle Solomon allowed him £160 a year, and Heine made about £120 by his writings. But in 1840 debts drove him to the mistake of accepting a pension of £16 a month from the French

Government under Guizot in recognition of his genius. I say mistake, because when the citizen-king fell in 1848, and Heine's enemies raised the usual howl at the discovery of the pension, he felt their onslaughts bitterly, not having the strength of our English Johnson to wish the pension had been twice as big, that they might have howled the more.

So the years went on. Heine was writing for French magazines his prose essays on the history of German thought, on the Romantic School, his Florentine Nights, and other things. Most of his works were published first in French. Even his poems appeared translated into French verse and prose. With the Germans in Paris, especially with the revolutionary exiles who swarmed there, he found it hard to remain on terms of intimacy. He abhorred their tobacco, their beer, their unfathomable incapacity. Like many apostles of liberty, he preferred to keep at a comfortable distance from the concrete human creatures for whom he preached. He had a fastidious and very proper horror of ill manners and grimy hands. Many feel the horror ; not so many remember that, if only the start were fair, these concrete human creatures might acquire manners as pretty as a diplomatist's, and hands as clean as a millionaire's.

Yet at heart Heine remained a German. To the last he steadily refused to be naturalized in France. On his grave he would have the words

written, " Here lies a German poet." In the midst
of Paris, far-off dreams came to him of the old
German land, the forests, the German tongue, the
quiet thought and dreamy passion which thinks on
yesterday and on to-morrow, but never grasps to-day.

> " Once I had a beautiful native land.
>   The oak grew there so high,
>   Violets softly nodded.
>   It was a dream.
> It kissed me in German, and in German
> (You can hardly believe how good it sounded)
>   It spoke the words, ' *Ich liebe dich.*'
>   It was a dream."

Or again—

> " When I, filled with the blessing of your kisses,
>   Lie happy in your arms,
>   Then you must never speak to me of Germany ;
>   I cannot bear it : I have my reasons.

> " I implore you, let Germany alone ;
>   You must not plague me with these eternal questions
>   Of home, of friends, and of the mode of life ;
>   I have my reasons : I cannot bear it.

> " The oaks are green, and blue are the eyes
>   Of German women ; they are eyes full of gentleness and
>   longing;
>   They sigh with love, and hope, and faith ;
>   I cannot bear it : I have my reasons."

So, like Tannhäuser on the Hill of Love, Heine began at last to yearn with unsatisfied heart for something, oh, how different from that Venusberg of Paris! About 1844 he paid two short visits to Hamburg, but, like Tannhäuser, he returned. The innumerable smile of Paris drew him back.

Two years later the last quatrain of the Heinesque lyric of his life began. It opened with a slight drooping of the left eyelid, and month by month the paralysis crept along its way. It took ten years to kill him. He at first attributed it to business cares. His cousin, whose life he had saved in the cholera time, robbed him, like a true son of Jacob, of the allowance which his rich uncle had wished to leave him. But his intimate friends and consolers always assured him that the disease was the natural and just penalty of an evil life, and with a fine cheerfulness Heine accepted their consolation. Little by little the eyelids closed; one eye went quite blind; the spinal marrow began to waste; the whole form shrank together. In 1848 he went for his last walk. He went, as was fitting, to the feet of the great goddess, the Venus of Milo, the embodiment of Hellenism. Then he entered that mattress grave —a cleft in six piled mattresses—which he never left, except when lifted out by women to be washed. For the most part alone with his wife, who called his silence a German conversation—alas! no man is a hero to the wife of his bosom—drugged with opium, fed like an unfledged bird, twisted into spirals by savage convulsions, his body covered with sores, his legs shrunk to threads of cotton— tortured by the pianos of school-girls and the visits of journalists, Heine, that incarnate Deity, that pleasure-loving apostle of Hellenism, that happy wandering student of old days, dragged on his life for eight years still.

All the time his spirit was invincible, his laughter and irony never failed. Some of his sayings are well known. When a girl visited him, he said, "Allow me to roll up the curtain of my eye to admire you." In the year of the Universal Exhibition he told the doctor his nervous system would take the gold medal for anguish. When the doctor asked if he could whistle (*siffler*), he said, "Alas, no, sir, not even at a tragedy by M. Scribe." Best of all, he never allowed his mother to suspect his illness. At night, in the hours of wakeful pain, he composed ballads, poems, and songs, which show no falling off in genius. It was as Théophile Gautier beautifully said, "The poet was nailed down alive in his coffin, but if you bent your ear over him, you heard the poetry singing, singing under the sable pall."

What heroism this implied may be seen from an account by Karl Hillebrand, who saw him just at the beginning of his illness (in 1849)—

"Heine was then already chained to his bed. His hearing had suffered. His eyes were always shut, except when with great effort his wasted finger lifted a weary eyelid. His legs were crippled and powerless. Every morning a mulatto woman lifted him on to a chair whilst his bed was made. He could not endure the service of a man. He could not bear the smallest noise. His pain was so terrible that he had to take morphia in three forms in order to get any rest at all, and then it was four hours' sleep at the most."

Or take a passage from one of Heine's own letters when the end was approaching (to St. René Taillandier, 1855)—

"My forefathers belonged to the Jewish religion. I was never proud of this origin, but certainly I have never gloried in being a Lutheran. . . . I used to feel myself humiliated at having to pass for a common human being, whereas the philosopher Hegel made me believe I was a God. How proud I was of my godhead then! What ideas I had of my greatness! It was a grand time, and only with sorrow can I think of it now that I lie stretched pitiably on my back. My disease takes frightful strides."

In his brief "Confessions," probably the last prose he ever wrote, he admits half ironically that he was returning to a kind of Deism almost Hebraic. I do not think that in Heine we ever find what we properly mean by religion ; nor should a man be judged by his final state, when pain and the gradual approach to death have unconsciously perverted or coloured his reason. Still, it is certain that Heine found a sense of repose, a childlike comfort, in meditating on that "dear God" of his childhood.

Of the Hegelian Pantheism he now said that it was too chilly to entice a dog from the hearth ; it could not kill a cat, much less a God. It was a restful relief to think that perhaps the dear God was left him still.

"In my grievous sickness," he writes, "it is a real mercy that there is some one left in heaven to whom without ceasing I can mutter the litany of my woes : especially after midnight, when Mathilde has gone to her much-needed rest. Praise God ! at such times I am not alone, but I can pray and entreat as much as I like without feeling abashed, and I can unfold all my heart before the Almighty, and entrust to him many secrets which we keep hidden even from our wives."

"As to my health," he writes in a letter, "I spend much time in prayer, and that's always a bad sign."

There is the same mixture of faith and irony in the "Book of Lazarus," *e.g.* in the twenty-fourth poem—

"O God, shorten my torment,
    So that I may be buried soon :
Thou knowest that I have no talent
    For martyrdom.

"Thou must permit me, O Lord,
    To marvel at Thy inconsistency :
Thou didst create the cheerfullest of poets,
    And now Thou robbest him of his good spirits.

" Pain dulls the cheery mind,
    And makes me melancholy ;
If the pitiful farce does not end,
    I shall become a Catholic at last.

" Then I will raise my howl to Thy ears
    Like other good Christians all—
O miserere ! the best of the humorists
    Is lost, is lost."

And there is the same irony in Heine's last
recorded words. A few hours before his death, a
zealous friend came bustling into the room to ask
how he stood with God. "Calm yourself," said the
dying hero. "God will pardon me. That's His
trade."

So he died, looking over the gay throng in the
Elysian Fields of Paris. He had wished that his
wife should marry again, so that one man at least
might regret his death. But she did not marry. I
remember her dying, not many years ago (in 1883).
She was very stout herself, and was devoted heart
and soul to two very stout dogs.

Certainly when God plagiarises Heine, He does
not do it by halves. There is only one fault in the
poem. I think the poet whose words are the lives
of men had forgotten that brevity is the soul of wit.
Ten years' torment was too long for that final stanza,
too long even for a poet of eternity. I am sure that
Heine himself would have cut it shorter.

We have lately been passing through a slack and

half-hearted time. The powers of darkness seem
within the last few years to have been regaining
ground. They have taken up positions from which
we thought they had been driven for ever. We
have seen many enthusiasms die. People have got
tired and fallen away, impatient because the battle
was not won at the first shout. Many are exhausted,
many are bored, most object to being unfashionable.
The old battle-cries have become tedious as the call
of " Old clo' " down the street. As long as it does
not touch their domestic comforts, people are easily
content with the *status quo,* and quixotic honour is
dismissed with a smile, so that it has seemed as if
things were going badly for the knights of the Holy
Spirit.

At such a time it is good to remember Heine's
unflinching part in the War of Liberation. "We
may not be much happier for cleaving to reason," he
wrote in his youth, "but at least we know that a
happiness due to a lie is no real happiness." And
in one of his latest poems he returns to his favourite
metaphor of a soldier resisting the hosts of darkness.
It is called "Enfant Perdu."

> " For thirty years I loyally held
>   A lost position in the war of freedom.
>   I fought without hope of victory,
>   I knew I never should get safe home.
>
> " By day and night I kept my watch—
>   I could not sleep like my friends in camp

D

(The mere snoring of those honest fellows
　　Kept me awake if ever I felt a bit drowsy).

" In those nights I was often overcome by weariness,
　　Often by fear (only fools fear nothing).
To drive away fear, I took to whistling
　　The audacious rhymes of my satires.

" Yes.   I stood wakeful, with my rifle ready,
　　And if any suspicious fool came near
I took good aim, and drove a fine warm bullet
　　Bang into his miserable belly.

" Sometimes, it's true, it might so happen
　　That the poor knave knew how to shoot
Just as well as I.   Alas ! I can't deny it—
　　My wounds are gaping, my blood is running away.

" A sentry-post is vacant—my wounds are gaping—
　　One falls, the others take his place.
Yet I fall unconquered, and my weapons
　　Are still unbroken ; it was only my heart that broke."

Let us remember Heine as that sentry of the
Holy Spirit, dying at his post, and let us think of
his quixotic contests, his passion for reason, his
unflagging gaiety, his tenderness in love and sorrow,
and that irresistible laughter which is after all a
weapon far more powerful than violence for dissolving
the bonds and formulæ of dulness.

Goethe's Birthday

A HUNDRED and fifty years to-day since Goethe was born—Goethe, in so many ways the type of the nineteenth century's thought and life. To what a distance the date takes us back! Pope had then only been five years dead. Johnson was just beginning his dictionary. The Hanoverian Government were trying to stifle the last echoes of "Charlie is my darling," and were wondering why no mortal ever made a darling of a Georgie. The elder Pitt was a rising young minister. The masterpieces of Goldsmith and Sterne were yet to be written. And in Germany, Frankfurt, where Goethe was born, still kept all the features of a mediæval town. There the electors still gathered with all the pageantry of the Middle Ages to choose an emperor of the world as Christ's temporal vicar here on earth. The city was confined within its ramparts and walls and ditches. Early in the evening the gates were shut, and the Jews barricaded into their fitting quarter. Emblazoned coaches lumbered through the land, and if they stuck all night in the mire, there were no

35

papers to write to with complaints. Frederick had not begun his Seven Years' War. German literature did not exist, and in that region of the inane Gottsched ruled supreme. Those are points which fairly mark the birthday of the poet and man of science who was to see the Napoleonic era transform Europe, to realize the social significance of railways and steam, to lay the foundations of the theory of evolution, to outlive Byron and Shelley, to be familiar with the first-fruits of Victor Hugo, and foretell the eminence of Carlyle. To few men is it granted to live through an age of transition so rapid and astonishing.

But the unique interest of Goethe's life lies just in that transition. He is the bridge from another age to our own. Belonging to both, and equally set in the earlier and later times, he carries us, as it were, across a gulf of extraordinary change. In his career the whole thought of the age is reflected. From stage to stage he followed every movement of the world, where he did not himself lead it. Each of his works and every point of his life is representative of an epoch such as is rarely witnessed among mankind. He grew with the rapid growth of the years. "I have always been like a snake," he used to say. "I cast my slough, and start afresh."

As a creative artist perhaps he does not stand quite so high as when all the world was reading

"Werther," or when the fragments of "Faust" filled the poets of Europe with astonishment. Probably few Englishmen read him now with the enthusiastic hope which Carlyle's early writings inspired for at least one generation. It is true that in the most barren of his fifty volumes the literary scavenger may still light upon jewels of wisdom, the brighter for their unexpectedness. But in the writings of a man whose interests were so wide there is inevitably much of only temporary value. There is much, too, that is chilled by German pedantry and that stiff "privy-councillor" style at which even Germans laugh, though they endure tedium with pathetic meekness. Intensely observant in art and criticism though he was, it is seldom that Goethe's works reach the true perfection of art itself. Think of "Meister," how the first part sprawls over its volumes, and the second part has about as much artistic value as a shot load of bricks. But when we have said the very worst that can be said—when we have recognized his temptation to diffuseness, his tendency to fragments, and a peculiar solemnity in dealing with subjects which, to most of us, appear little less trivial than a collector's hobbies—we must then remember that, after all, we are dealing thus lightly with one of the chief creative intellects of the world. This was the man who conceived the anguished passion of "Werther" and the passionate happiness of the "Roman Elegies." He was the

poet of songs which even Heine declared to be the
sweetest ever sung.   Here is the creator of Philine,
the child of earth, and of the " Beautiful Soul," the
bride of heaven, and of Mignon, the spirit of the
south, and Gretchen, the supreme example of
human pathos, and Wagner, the type of learned
stupidity, and Faust, the unappeased and restless
soul of modern mankind, and Mephisto, the modern
devil, one of the most profoundly significant figures
in all creative art.   Those are poems and living
characters which have passed into the general heritage of man.   After all, the achievement is not
bad.

It is often said that Goethe's public life at
Weimar hindered his creative power.   It sometimes
seems as though he sold his birthright for a mess of
aristocratic society.   That is partly true.   As he
says in " Meister," " Action animates, but narrows."
But then it was exactly the animation of action
which literature at that time needed, and perhaps
always needs.   Certainly he did not go to court for
a life of leisure.   He administered that little state
as few states were ever administered.   By turns or
together he was Minister of Finance, of Education,
and of War, Director of Mines, Roads, and the
Theatre, to say nothing of his frequent labours at
night as fireman among the poor wooden villages of
the forest side.   It was by this keen occupation with
the realities of life that he gave a new power and

value to literature and to thought, saving them from
the sentimentality and vague emotion of the time.
Life and truth always occupied his mind more than
the production of books or poems such as the
tender hearts of Germany demanded of him. In
the " Venetian Epigrams " he cries —

" Ah yes, the tender hearts ! Any bungler is able to touch
them.
My one prayer is to touch, Nature, the hem of thy robe."

From first to last he was on the side of sanity—a
standing proof that genius is not necessarily a morbid
growth. Capable in . body of every hardship and
fatigue, he lived to eighty-three, and the illness he
died of was only his fourth. But his contact with
external life gave him also a characteristic sanity of
mind. He gained from it something of that " severe
delight " which Wordsworth gained from his simplicity. His life and art were so commingled that,
like lovers, each borrowed the quality of the other,
the one giving charm and the other reality. " In all
my works," he used to say, " I have never shammed
(*nie affectirt*)." And so we find embodied in them
or scattered through their pages that " holy seriousness " which, as the youths sang over Mignon's
body, alone gives life eternity. When we remember
how this " seriousness "—this refusal to sham or
take things lightly and at second-hand—guided the
poet's own.career through almost every conceivable

phase of human life with all human virtues and human sins—we see that to him may be applied the song which the angels sang as they bore Faust's body up to heaven, " Who strenuously onward strives, him we have power to redeem."

" *Sweetness and Light* "

I T was Matthew Arnold's habit, as his daughter
tells us in her brief preface to his " Note-
books," to keep for each year a narrow
little book, and in it to jot down his various
engagements and, what was more important, any
short and striking sentence which he came across
during his daily reading, or which he recalled as
suitable to his mood. The notebooks extended
over thirty-seven years, and in the published volume
we are given only a very brief selection. For
far the greater part of them, the quotations for
each fifth year only have been printed, but it is
strange with what exactness this mere collection of
other people's thoughts (for his own are never in-
truded) reproduces for us the portrait of the mind
which made it. The most obvious feature is, not so
much the breadth, as the height, of his reading.
Here we see with what strictness he followed his
own maxim that it is the business of criticism to
know and make known the best that is known and
thought in the world. It may be said that, like
nearly all educationalists, Matthew Arnold exaggerated the importance of books and reading as a means
of culture. True culture has often been reached

without a knowledge of the alphabet, but Matthew
Arnold certainly placed the importance of reading
very high. A few years before his death he wrote
to his sister—

> "The importance of reading, not slight stuff to get
> through the time, but the best that has been written, forces
> itself upon me more and more every year I live ; it is living
> in good company, the best company, and people are generally
> quite keen enough, or too keen about doing that, yet they
> will not do it in the simplest and best manner by reading.
> However, if I live to be eighty I shall probably be the only
> person left in England who reads anything but newspapers
> and scientific publications."

There we come upon the characteristic note. He
may or may not have overvalued reading as a means
of culture. Certainly it does not necessarily lead to
sweetness and light. The average German professor,
though he has read more than any other human
being, is not conspicuously luminous or sweet. But
then, in all his acute sayings and illuminating defini-
tions, Matthew Arnold always had his eye upon
England, and in England reading never seemed
likely to be driven to excess. Certainly not that
austere intellectual exercise which alone he would
have counted as reading—the mental devotion and
asceticism essential for the knowledge of the best
that is known and thought in the world. In England
people read a great deal, far more than in conversa-
tional countries like France or Spain, but they read

to pass time, or, as we brutally but accurately call it, to " kill " time. They regard reading as a sedative, the easiest and most relaxing exercise which can keep the mind just conscious of employment. It is the English substitute for chloral, and creates a similar craving. But the reading that Matthew Arnold followed—the " industrious and select reading " spoken of by Milton—was a very different matter.

In considering the extracts entered in the notebooks, we notice, as we said, a height rather than any remarkable extent of reading. Nearly all the quotations come from well-worn books that any one may know. They belong to catholic literature, to books universally recognized, to the best that has been thought. Probably the greatest number come from the best books in the Bible, especially the Psalms and St. Paul's letters. Next to these stand the best writers of Greece—Plato and the tragedians. From literature since the time of Christ, Goethe's wise sayings are perhaps the most numerous. But there is much from the " Imitation," much from the French, and a good deal from our old friend Bishop Wilson, almost the only little-known thinker whom Arnold persistently quoted—a man so little known that Huxley believed him to be a literary Mrs. Harris, a person who never was. The quotations cover all manner of subjects. They even contain one joke. But if a general principle can be traced, we should say it was an exhortation to definite and constant labour—to work that " fills and moralizes the day," as Arnold was fond of quoting from a noble French sentence. The Latin precept, " Always set before yourself some definite aim," recurs more often than any other, and the two main conditions of all good work—isolation and limitation—are also constantly insisted upon. To disregard the transient and trivial, and to serve the eternal alone—it is strange to see with what persistency the poet braces himself up to that exacting standard. That lucidity of thought, that temper of intellect, clear almost to coldness, was not won without a discipline as rigorous as a monk's. Time after time we find repeated the warnings, not only against such bodily pleasures as blunt the soul, but against the casual interests that split and distract it. That sharp edge of intellect along which he seemed to move so easily was not reached or held without continuous effort. Remembering how calm and self-assured the poet always seemed—a little " superior," perhaps a little supercilious—we had sometimes wondered at the verses beginning—

> " The thoughts that rain their steady glow
> 　Like stars on life's cold sea,
> Which others know, or say they know—
> 　They never shone for me."

If any one was illumined by a steady glow of

star-like thoughts, we should have supposed it was
Matthew Arnold.   But the notebook shows with
what elaborate and unfailing care those white fires
had to be fed.

There is very little change of tone throughout
the book ; after intervals of fifteen or twenty years
the same passages are frequently repeated.   By
about thirty-five the mind was formed, and it did
not vary much again, though in the later years,
perhaps, the exhortations to cheerfulness and amia-
bility are more pronounced ; the way of peace, the
belief that shows itself in patience, is more often
referred to.   We find the great text, " He that
believeth shall not make haste ; " we find Goethe's
saying—

" He that would do good work must never scold, must
never trouble himself about the unfitness of things, but
simply go on doing good work."

Or again, there is the passage, perhaps from
Renan, and certainly characteristic of him, as it was
of Arnold himself—

" Pour gagner l'humanité, il faut lui plaire ; pour lui
plaire, il faut être aimable."

Or, again, the exquisite simile—

" Oh that thou hadst hearkened unto my commandments !
then had thy peace been as a river."

These were among his thoughts as he drew

towards old age—that old age of the soul which he
so deeply dreaded, and from which sudden death
happily delivered him. But sudden as his death
was, he seems to have felt a strange foreboding of it.
Against the Sunday on which he died, he had
written ahead in his notebook this verse from Eccle-
siastes—

"Weep bitterly over the dead, as he is worthy, and then
comfort thyself; drive heaviness away ; thou shalt not do
him good, but hurt thyself."

And for the following Sunday—the Sunday
after his burial—he had written—

"When the dead is at rest, let his memory rest ; and be
comforted for him when his spirit is departed from him."

He could hardly have chosen better epitaphs for
himself, unless he had taken that promise of peace
as a river to him that keeps the eternal Commandments. Critics who lightly dismiss Matthew Arnold
as a Greek mind appearing in un-Hellenic days, do
injustice to a character which strove with religious
diligence to make its culture a "study of perfection."
They remain blind to the very side which Arnold
himself always declared to be the most important
of any. His notebook's constant references to
"Thy Law," as it is understood in the Psalms, and
to the principle of eternity, which he almost identifies

with the same Law, are proof of his lifelong occupation with conduct—with what he liked to call
Hebraism. But there again comes in that characteristic we noticed above. Keeping his eye always
fixed on England, he found that in England there is
a strong tendency to exaggerate this Hebraism (the
word is not satisfactory, but he has made it familiar)
to the exclusion of knowledge, to the exclusion of
" sweetness and light ; " and so it blocked the path
of culture, which is " the harmonious expansion of
all the powers which make the beauty and worth of
our human nature." He saw that the strictness
of conscience inculcated by " Hebraism " was not
preventing our aristocracy from becoming, as he used
to say, materialized barbarians, or our middle classes
from becoming vulgarized Philistines, or our working-
classes from becoming a brutalized populace. And
it was for this reason that he insisted upon the
" sweetness and light," the " sweet reasonableness,"
for which the English as a race did not appear to be
distinguished. For this reason he advocated the
" free play of consciousness " around an abuse or
proposal of reform rather than the far easier belief in
" machinery," which is the besetting sin of English
political thought. Greatness, he saw, has nothing
to do with commerce or coal or iron or wealth in
any form. Greatness has nothing to do with
" machinery," whether political or social. " Greatness is a spiritual condition worthy to excite love,

interest, and admiration," and it was at that spiritual
condition that he himself aimed throughout a life of
rigorous endeavour and almost inhuman restraint.
Inhuman ? Well, his books won for him interest,
they won for him admiration, but has any one on
their account given him " the greatest of these
three " ?

The Philosophic Mind

SOME fifty-five years after the Crucifixion the Laodicean Greek, Epictetus, who in Rome had once been a slave to one of Nero's most shameless favourites, and had just been driven from the city in common with all other "philosophers" as a danger or a bore, came to the town of Nicopolis, which Augustus built on the bay of Actium in memory of the victory that made him master of the world. There, looking over the narrow sea where, hardly more than a century before, Antony had turned from the fight to follow the Serpent of old Nile, he spent the rest of his life discoursing on morality and behaviour to such young men as came to listen. They could hardly have been very many, for the place was outside the current of the world. If a man sought wisdom he would naturally rather go to Athens, only three or four days' journey off, where for over five hundred years all wisdom had made her home; if he wanted worship, he would go to Delphi, over the Achelous and the spurs of Pindus; and if he wanted consecrated athletics, he would cross the gulf and pass through Elis to Olympia. Though her true life was long over, at no time had Greece been more radiant in outward beauty ; at no time had her ritual been richer, and her schools and temples better patronized by the wealthy and official classes of the world. Epictetus himself speaks of natural man's longing to be in Athens or at Olympia, just as a Canadian professor might speak of a colonial's longing to be at Oxford or the Oaks. And no doubt the longing was his own. Yet we would rather imagine him making his way along the track where now the Turkish road runs from Preveza up to Janina, and after a long day's ride reaching that most ancient shrine of Zeus among the trees of Dodona. He would find a few priests there still maintaining the immemorial religion in its purity, and still hearing the voice of the god himself among the rustling leaves. In such a scene, he might, at least as truly as Matthew Arnold at the Grande Chartreuse, have used the famous words—

> " Wandering between two worlds, one dead,
> The other powerless to be born,
> With nowhere yet to rest my head,
> Like these, on earth I wait forlorn."

Stoicism is the mood of good men who wait between two worlds. It is not religion ; it has no inspiration ; it almost implies regret for the loss of religion. It is not even philosophy, for it sets aside speculation and is concerned almost entirely with conduct. It appears at crises when the accepted sanctions of virtue are shaken, and the leaders of society's thinking are discovering with relief that, as the sanctions are uncertain, the virtues do not matter ; as though at a king's death all his laws were abrogated. Then comes the Stoic with his desperate and unyielding belief in the supreme excellence of virtue apart from all the sanctions of divinity or tradition. So far from virtue being of no matter, to him it is the only thing that counts. The moral will, the choice of good or evil, is man's supreme faculty. To the man who chooses aright, no evil can happen either in life or death, and the virtuous life is the life according to nature—the life in which the special lines laid down by nature for a man, a woman, or a horse, are most rigidly followed, without considerations of profit, pleasure, or external authority. Against the Stoic the tyranny either of fashion or force is impotent ; "If you choose," says Epictetus, "you are free." No fortune touches him ; one who had lost all he had, could quietly say, "No evil has befallen me." No external power can rob you of your will. When some one complained to Epictetus, "My brother ought not to have treated me thus," he replied, "True, but *he* must see to that." To the righteous there is no prison, to the sinner the only prison is to abide in his sin. To the good man it is no evil to be torn in half on the rack, and if when his son has died, he be asked what evil has happened to himself, he

will reply, " None." With the good man's happiness
the events of the outside world have no concern ;
" To me," said Epictetus, " there is neither robber
nor earthquake."

It is magnificent. It is the apotheosis of the
wrestling angel in man. The Stoic is generally said
to have held the duality of man's nature in its
extreme form ; but in fact the bodily side almost
disappears under his enthusiasm for the spirit. It
was this that made Socrates " bear himself as a
kinsman of the gods ; " this that almost transformed
Seneca from a humbug ; this that taught Marcus
Aurelius the possibility of virtue even in a palace ;
this that vibrated in the " iron string " of Emerson,
and fixed Matthew Arnold's meditation on " the
Eternal," and speaks again in Maeterlinck's "Sagesse."
In Epictetus it took on a gentle cheerfulness, an
amenity, that makes us welcome the more the little
volume of " Golden Sayings " which Mr. Hastings
Crossley has admirably prepared, as well as a new
edition of George Long's version of the " Discourses."
Though he speaks of the Cynics with veneration, and
almost identifies his doctrines with theirs, there was
no touch of what we now call cynicism in his nature.
He regarded the cynic life as a counsel of perfection
in a naughty world ; much as a cultivated Roman
Catholic now regards the life of the early Franciscans.
But to Epictetus the good man is not severed from
his kind, though he keeps himself unspotted from

the world. He advises his pupils to go through the ordinary stages of existence—to marry, to beget children, to follow public life, to fulfil the offices of citizenship. He directs them not to be like a traveller who, instead of returning to his country and his duties at home, hangs about at random inns upon the road for his own pleasure. He tells them to avoid the outward appearance of asceticism —not to appear unto men to fast—and is himself peculiarly careful in matters of cleanliness and decent dress and general social behaviour. "Try," he says, "to enjoy the great festival of life with other men." Those who cannot enjoy it he adjures nevertheless to abide at their post like sentries, as Socrates had taught, and it must have been only in a moment of desponding weakness that he reminded them for their comfort how the door to death always stands open. For his own part, he is resolutely cheerful— nay, he is joyous at moments. In an early chapter of the first book of his "Discourses," as his pupil Arrian noted them down, he says—

"Whether digging or ploughing or eating, should we not sing this hymn to God : 'Great is God, who has given us such implements to till the ground ; great is God, who has given us hands and the power of swallowing and digesting, and the power of unconsciously growing, and of breathing while we sleep'? What else can I do that am old and lame but sing to God ? Were I a nightingale, I should do as the nightingale ; were I a swan, I should do as the swan ; but as I am a reasonable being, I must sing to God.

That is my work : I will do it, nor desert my post as long
as it is granted me to hold it."

Of Stoicism on this side, too, we may say that it
is magnificent. It means more than what Carlyle
meant by the "cheerful Stoicism" which he considered characteristic of the British aristocracy ; for
we have never heard an English baronet or even an
earl singing to God because he was a reasonable
being. In practice it comes very near to the choice
and cleanly Epicureanism of Walter Pater's Marius.
It is a noble attempt to inspire the most rigid form
of virtue with freedom and life, and to enshrine a
rose among the symbols of mortality. Inevitably it
calls to mind the great verse in Wordsworth's Ode
to Duty, beginning—

> "Stern Lawgiver ! yet thou dost wear
>   The Godhead's most benignant grace ;
> Nor know we anything so fair
>   As is the smile upon thy face."

But in spite of this benignant grace, in spite of this
solemn beauty that is so nearly divine, why is it,
then, that the mention of Stoicism gives poor mankind the shivers, as though a superior person were
walking over our graves ? When we speak of
Stoics, even of such an affable and benign type as
Epictetus, we seem to see a procession of grey forms,
enveloped in togas, stalking unmoved through this
dirty puddle of a world, and betraying their mental

torture only by the fixity of their smile. We
know they are good men and true, we know
they follow virtue, and would be turned from
their path by no anguish and no form of death.
We know they alone stand for righteousness when
she is sorely beset. We should know all that,
even if they were not continually mentioning the
fact. We know also that they want to be nice to us
and not to put themselves in any way above their
fellow-men. We hear them imploring each other
to try to enjoy life with other people—as if that
were a mighty difficult task! When we meet them
they manufacture a laugh, and set themselves with
superhuman effort to be pleasant, like philanthropists
entertaining the poor with educational games in
the East End. For all this we are grateful, for
we can imagine what the effort must cost them.
We recognize their virtue. In the slight chilliness
and melancholy of their demeanour we see the mood
of good men wandering between two worlds. We
admire their positivism—the constancy with which
they refuse to be put off with any fond dream that
the laws of reason and arithmetic will not allow.
We admire their "passionate coldness." But as
poor bedraggled and bespattered mortals, we take
leave to remark that it is a passionate warmth rather
than coldness that moves the sun and the other
stars. Why is it that unreasoning mankind, in its
sin and joy and weariness, may be said to love little

St. Francis, but has never loved the Emperor Marcus ? Or what is the immense difference between a chapter of à Kempis and a chapter of Epictetus ? To bear a thing "philosophically," to cultivate the "philosophic mind," to offer the condolence of "philosophy"—there is something unreal, untrue, and abhorrent in it all—something at which man's nature shivers or laughs. Stoicism had all the virtues. We treat it with honour and respect ; we do it reverence, and we pass. It is magnificent, but it is not peace.

The Last of the Prophets

THE worst of a series like the " English Men of Letters " is that it demands a book, whether the book is wanted or not. There was no call for another biography of Ruskin, apart from the necessities of the series. Everything that is worth knowing about him he has told us himself, and with a mingling of irony and simplicity so charming that no biographer's attempt can equal it. Indeed, all his books are so strangely full of his personality that they form an almost unbroken record of his life from year to year till his writing ceased and there was no more to tell. Every change of mood, every growth of opinion, every discovery of further truth, is woven into that gorgeous tapestry. And there, too, if we choose, we may find in nearly complete sequence the mere external events with which common biography deals—the places of education, the changes of home, the worldly fortunes, the foreign travels, the friendships, loves, and estrangements, that do to some small extent influence a great spirit, however powerfully its own nature may have predestined its course.

Those who have not the time or the mind to follow the story in the works themselves, could either leave the subject alone, or turn to Mr. Collingwood's "Life" and many other excellent guides, aids, selections, and biographical notices which lie within easy reach. But in a series of "English Men of Letters," it was impossible to omit the man whom probably every one would place among the first six of English last-century writers. It was impossible to omit the man who used our language with so superb a power, whether for the strictest analysis of criticism and science, or for the expression of every note of human emotion, from savage indignation to the winning endearments of a tired or happy child. So the series has given us the book, and we do not in the least regret it.

Mr. Frederic Harrison's qualifications for writing the biography lend his work a peculiar interest. Himself a personal friend of Ruskin, he is always on the verge of being carried away into whole-hearted devotion. Himself endowed with a high sense for beauty, and capable of style, he is almost overcome by a master so full of the revelation of beauty, and by the record of a life generously free from self-interest and devoted without reserve to the highest aims. But in the glow of his admiration comes the chilling thought that after all this is not the master to whom his allegiance is due ; and, what is worse, that this master spent some of his time in laughing at the other, and in meeting solemn phrases about "the sense of collective evolution," with appeals to the results of " separate evolution," which ought to have made him handsomer than the Elgin Theseus, but perhaps had not ! And so Mr. Harrison becomes a little flustered, and goes fluttering about the Positivist library to prove that all Ruskin's best things had already been said by Auguste Comte before him. His main contention in economics, we are told, had " never before been stated so boldly and so dogmatically, except by Auguste Comte." The plea in " King's Treasuries " against wasting time in the reading of valueless books is "exactly the aim of Auguste Comte when he published, in 1851, his ' Positivist Library for the Nineteenth Century.'" And the famous passage in " Queen's Gardens " defining woman's sphere is framed "almost exactly in the words used by Comte many years before."

Such deliberate loyalty is the more amiable because Mr. Harrison is continually torn between his instinctive perception of charm and his sectarian duty to Positivist science and mechanical progress— just the kind of things which Ruskin fretted his soul away in combating. From time to time we find him driven by the dignity of his Positivist position to chide the master as a school dame might chide a wayward and dreamy boy who employed his astonishing imagination in devising fresh booby-traps for respectable citizens. The criticism upon

the Oxford lectures on Leighton and Tadema is one
long scold, and yet the upshot of those lectures was
no whimsical caprice ; it was the logical and inevitable
consequence of all Ruskin's previous teaching on art.
Some passages in Mr. Harrison's book even make
one doubt whether, with all his knowledge and love
of Ruskin's works, he has ever penetrated to the
principles of his criticism at all. Take the following
comment on a very familiar type of sentence :—

> "'There is no instance' (said Ruskin) 'of fine sculpture
> being produced by a nation, either torpid, weak, or in
> decadence. Their drama may gain in grace and wit ; but
> their sculpture in days of decline is always base.' *Cela donne
> à réflêchir*, when we remember that the model for Paraxiteles'
> Aphrodite was Phryne, and that Michael Angelo worked
> for the popes and princes of the sixteenth century."

So far from having to reflect over these two
instances as contradictions to Ruskin's rule, any
student of his works would at once reply that they
are exactly such examples as prove it. It was
exactly the degeneracy seen in the work of Praxiteles
compared to the heroic age of Greece, or in the
work of Michael Angelo compared to the spiritual
age of Italy, which Ruskin connected with the social
decadence that produced Phryne and the popes and
princes of the sixteenth century. He may have
been right, or he may have been wrong, but Mr.
Harrison's contradictory instances, so far from
startling us, sound like the very commonplaces of

Ruskin criticism. When Mr. Harrison sets himself to lecture the old teacher and consummate artist upon questions of art, or when, fuming over some economic paradox, he exclaims that to dispute the righteousness of interest would destroy the bases of civilization, one longs for a touch of that vanished hand which, one May-time a quarter of a century ago, wrote the open letter beginning—

"MY DEAR HARRISON,—I am very glad you have been enjoying yourself at Oxford, and that you still think it a pretty place."

One longs for the irresistible irony with which that hand would have answered Mr. Harrison's scoldings, and certainly Mr. Harrison longs for it too. Not that he is particularly fond of irony himself. Like many people not gifted with a full sense of proportion, he is rather puzzled and irritated at its stealthy and delicate approach, and is more at ease when facts and deductions are set down in solid solemnity without a smile. But then his regretful affection for the perverse and enchanting master is so genuine! Time after time it bursts through all the melancholy restrictions of Positivist science and economic propriety, and the rigid school dame of one page whispers to us on the next, "Bless his little heart! Was ever such a boy!" Thus we read—

"The ninety-six letters of 'Fors' contain the tale of a

long career of failures, blunders, and cruel disappointment.
They contain, too, the record of that damning perversity of
mind and of character which ruined Ruskin's life and
neutralized his powers, the folly of presuming to recast the
thought of humanity *de novo*, and alone ; to remould civilization by mere passion without due training or knowledge ;
attempting alone to hurl human society back into a wholly
imaginary and fictitious past."

And a line or two lower down comes the caressing
forgiveness—

" But there are some failures more beautiful and more
useful to mankind than a thousand triumphs. It is impossible to weigh the value or to judge the legitimacy of a
hopeless but heroic sacrifice. . . . In things social and
religious it is the fervour of belief, the loathing of falsehood,
the abandonment of every self-interested and even of every
prudential motive, which tells in the end. Magnanimity
owes no account of its acts to prudence. No ; nor to
common sense."

It is superb. It is the passionate word of the
true disciple, full of his master's spirit. And it is in
sharp contrasts like this that the chief interest of
Mr. Harrison's book lies.

Of course, there is much else. The usual facts
and dates of biography are given, and wherever Mr.
Harrison speaks from personal memory of his own
intercourse with the man or their common labour in
the Working Men's College, the quality of biography
rises. His descriptions of Ruskin's outward personality are exactly right. It would indeed be difficult

for the memory of so distinct a figure to become blurred, and to those who saw him walking up to his place in Christ Church choir Sunday after Sunday, or entering the Museum theatre for his lectures, the sight will always seem present. He chose to think of himself simply as an Oxford professor, but there was no professor in the least like him. As may be proved from my memory of the scene when he concluded one of his courses with words of such solemn beauty that, instead of applauding as usual, we sat there absolutely silent, hardly daring to breathe. Ruskin looked round for a moment as if puzzled, but feeling what had happened, he turned and made a quiet but jesting remark about some pictures on the wall, and then the spell was broken, and the applause seemed as if it could never end.

All this personal side is well done in Mr. Harrison's book, though the unhappiness of the life is dwelt upon rather to excess. As human life goes, there is no need to dwell on the unhappiness of a man whose days were so full, whose spirit so alert, and who after all accomplished so extraordinary an amount of work as artist, writer, and leader of men. It is true that a mind so sensitive to beauty and joy was born into an age when what Mr. Harrison would call the Spirit of Humanity was for some reason or other passing through a period of peculiar hideousness and suffering. But, after all, he was in time to see the last traces of the beauty he best loved before they vanished from Europe; whilst he lived his teaching had some small but definite effect on his country's social life—a rare reward for a prophet; and death saved him just in time from the sight of motor-cars booming and stinking along our lanes. "Who hath believed our report?" is the common cry of prophets, and their common sorrow. But in the case of Ruskin many believed, and something in the end was gained. One is grateful to Mr. Harrison, at all events, for not raising the common cry of "pessimist," because a man's vision of life's possibilities and dues are higher and brighter than the average citizen's. Speaking of the stern denunciations in some of Ruskin's later work, he writes—

"Nothing has been uttered more fierce, more pathetic by Swift or Rousseau, by Byron or Carlyle. But in the groans of Ruskin there is no trace of personal shame, of wounded vanity, of cynicism, or of despair. It is the torture endured by a tender spirit, morbidly outraged at the sight of grossness and cruelty; it is a noble rage against vulgarity and wrong; a resurrection of the mediæval godliness of St. Francis and à Kempis, in a world which had no place for those saintly ecstasies."

But it is not with the idea of saintly ecstasies in our minds that we should take leave of a man like Ruskin. Underlying his wildest visions and most paradoxical laments was the perfectly solid basis of practical truth. When all is said, the heart of all his long endeavour lay in the discovery—not so very startling or ecstatic, one would have thought—that the workman is of more importance than the work, and that, as far as beauty goes, it is no good painting pretty pictures and talking about art as long as the life of most people is spent in dreary or disgusting ugliness, and the usual accompaniment of growth and progress is the poisoning or disfigurement of nature. Those propositions appear sane enough, and indeed it was the sanity of his work more even than its imaginative charm which gave him his power. Perhaps that is why the last words I ever heard him speak have always remained so clearly in my mind. It was during his last journey abroad, in the midst of the mountains he loved best. "There are, of course, good people still," he said to me with his half-smile, "but they seem to spend all their time in undoing the harm the others have done—in nursing, reforming the East End, teaching idiots, and so on, while the healthy and hopeful are neglected. But it is the sane, and not the sick, who are best worth working for." When hurried people talk of Ruskin as an impracticable madman who wrote good prose, it is pleasant to remember such words.

The Last of Romances

" THE Sundering Flood " is the sixth and
last of the prose tales of pure
imagination which Morris gave us
towards the end of his life, and we find
in it all the well-known characteristics. The scene is
again laid in the land and age that never were. We
may, indeed, vaguely call them mediæval, for the
dress, the buildings, the decoration, the fighting, and
the mode of life are pretty much the kind of thing
which the Middle Ages are fondly supposed to have
supplied. But the spirit of the people among whom
we are transported has in reality little more to do
with mediæval history than the peculiar language
which they speak. To take one instance, the whole
of the Christian religion, which undoubtedly exercised
some influence on mediæval life, is here entirely
omitted ; for though we hear of monastery and Mass
and church, and sometimes come upon an appeal to
Rood and Virgin, these things are introduced but as
decorative additions to the scenery. They are the
æsthetic trimmings borrowed from a faith which
promoted the arts and crafts. Of the faith itself we
have no trace whatever. What little religion comes
in at all belongs rather to the fairy-lore or giant

myths of old Iceland or the Northmen, and the spiritual powers we are really asked to believe in are the dwarfs, the witch carlines, and dim warrior figures who come with gifts of magic sword and bow. There is, in fact, something of the Saga about the tone of the romances, though in this, the latest of them, the resemblance to Malory, and even to some of the early chroniclers, is perhaps more marked.

But if the actual world never in the least corresponded to the picture here imagined, most of us would say that we only wish it did. For here are women most lovable, and men most generous and brave. The country is open and full of sweet air from mountains and sea. The habitations of men are few, but adorned with the simplest beauty of handicraft, and, above all, the unjust person or oppressor, when he does appear, is so easily and certainly overcome. Of this sweet country a map in the ancient style is given, showing on each side of the river, which is the Sundering Flood, a land of woods and desert waste and mountains and many pleasant hills where steads and cots and castles are. And at the mouth of this flood, beside the sea, stands a city fair and spacious, with towered walls, and a harbour meet for seafarers—

"Up this river ran the flood of a tide a long way, so that the biggest of dromonds and roundships might fare along it, and oft they lay amid pleasant up-country places, with their yards all but touching the windows of the husbandman's stead, and their bowsprits thrusting forth amongst the middens, and the routing swine, and querulous hens ; and the uneasy lads and lasses sitting at High Mass of the Sunday in the grey village church would see the tall masts dimly amidst the painted saints of the aisle windows, and their minds would wander from the mass-hackled priest and the words and the gestures of him, and see visions of far countries and outlandish folk, and some would be heart-smitten with that desire of wandering and looking on new things which so oft the sea-beat board and the wind-strained pine bear with the to them dwellings of the stay-at-homes.''

But the chief part of the story does not lie in this city, but far up the river near the mountains, at its source in the little home of Wethermel.   For here dwells Osberne, son of Wulfgrim, who is but a boy of twelve when we meet him first, yet of such courage and happy nature as likely to grow into " a man to be loved of women and to love them some-what overmuch.''   And so it fell out, though, indeed, his love was ever constant from the moment when first he met the lady most worth the loving.   For on a day when already he had won a good name for the slaying of the three great wolves and other adventure, he lit upon a maid tending sheep with unked pipe among the rocks.   Fair and sweet and scantily clad she was, albeit with limbs somewhat skinny, being still but a girl.   But woe betide ! how the full stream of the Sundering Flood boiled and raged between two hearts, so that neither might come near the other, nor was any bridge found but only two hundred miles away hard by the river's mouth. Still, on every third day the twain would come to that place and gaze across the water and make goodly love in word. And Osberne with his bow would shoot across as presents to her clasps and raiment and other small chaffer which he had got him from a carle, or in some cheaping-stead. Wore the time, nor may we stay to tell how the youngling received the great sword Board-Cleaver, and how therewith he smote the foeman Hardcastle, sending him noseling to the ground, and went to the wars against the Baron of Deepdale, whom also he stole away by night, and all the time he grew more hardy and more manlike, and the maiden's limbs less skinny. Yet could they not come beside each other, so that from longing they well-nigh fell into wan hope. Something of a scald was the youngling, too, and could smithy out staves, many of which are cast scattermeal about the book, and give us whipping cheer should we at any moment become sleep-eager in the tale. But let us rather read how he and his men felt at heart on coming back one day from the war. It is not, in sooth, the knop and ouch of it all, but in itself it is fair—

"When at last they had won through that rocky tangle and had opened Wethermel, and nought lay before them but the grassy slopes and the wide-spread valley cleft by the line of the Sundering Flood ; now, when they saw in the clear air the grey houses of Wethermel lying together, and the smoke of the evening cooking-fires going up to the heavens, and the sheep wending on, thick and huddling before the driving of three tall men, and the kine moving towards the byre, and the women amongst them, then this befell : that whereas they had been all of one mind that when they came to the crown of the bent they would spur on and race merrily toward Wethermel, yet now when it lay before them, and there was so little a way betwixt them and its hearth, they all of them with one consent drew rein and sat still on their horses, as if they had suddenly come face to face with the host of foemen."

But unhappily soon after that return the land westward of the flood, where the lovable Elfhild dwelt, was ravaged by other foemen and thrall-cheapers, and many a grim shot-stour had they with Osberne across the water. Indeed, they carried off the maid, and she came no more to the tryst. Then Osberne rode out into the world upon a way-beast to find her, and, taking service under a gallant knight, he fought in the wars against the great city, and his name and battle-cry of the Red Lad became famous through all the land. Yet in all his prowess he thought unceasingly upon Elfhild, and at the last, when both had wandered far and suffered many things, and he himself had been wounded nigh unto death by gangrel men, he happed by a witch carline's help upon a cot within a wood, and slew the three felons who came wantoning there—

"The two women stood looking toward the open door

the while, and the maiden said faintly and in a quavering
voice, ‘Mother, what is it ? What has befallen ? Tell me,
what am I to do?’ ‘Hush, my dear,’ said the carline,
‘hush ; it is but a minute’s waiting after all these years.’
Even therewith came a firm footstep to the door, and
Osberne stepped quietly over the threshold, bareheaded now,
and went straight to Elfhild ; and she looked on him, and
the scared look went out of her face, and nought but the
sweetness of joyful love was there. And he cried out : ‘O
my sweet, where is now the Sundering Flood ? ’ And there
they were in each other’s arms as though the long years had
never been.”

The book, though not by any means the noblest
piece of the Master’s work, is a worthy conclusion
of it. The story is much clearer and more direct
than the “Wondrous Isles,” and it is entirely free
from any puzzling suggestions of allegory of which
that romance had plenty. At the same time it loses
perhaps in the sense of mystery which fairy romance
demands. There is nothing really unked or ken-
speckle about it ; and furthermore, we had liefer be
in love with Birdalone of the “ Isles ” than with
Elfhild, gracious and loving though she is. The
story is indeed the life of a man, as the “ Isles ” was
of a woman, and as such there is little to wyte in it.
For in sooth if one called it a right good book, us
seemeth he were not over big-wordy, and we should
yeasay him. Moreover if some humble clerk at the
hour of bever goes to a cheaping-shop, and louting
low to the drudgling giveth him the sele of the day,

and asketh for this book, nor is debt-tough but draweth from his pouch the half of one silver mark, we do him to wit that belike he will make good catch ; for it is the Master's voidee-cup.

Wedded Genius

THE late Professor Froude began his career with a book called "The Nemesis of Faith," and now, long after that career is ended, there comes to us, in the "New Letters and Memorials of Jane Welsh Carlyle," a book that is intended as the Nemesis of Disbelief. His disbelief, we mean, in the noble and spotless character of the friend, the man of extraordinary genius, who trusted him with all the letters, reminiscences, and other materials to tell the story of a life so remarkable and exercising such incalculable influence upon the course of English thought.

Twenty-two years have now passed since Carlyle's death. Froude issued the two volumes of "Reminiscences" almost at once, the "Early Life" in 1882, the "Letters of Mrs. Carlyle" in 1883, and the final volumes of the "Life in London" in 1885. Every one who then cared for literature will remember the abhorrent turmoil which these volumes created. Never did an admiring biographer perform so ill a service for his hero, and for his heroine too. The lives of two of the most sensitive and reserved of mortals were exposed in pitiless detail. They were turned inside out before the public gaze. They were paraded naked along the streets of Askelon. In the intervals of their interest in the " Bitter Cry of Outcast London " and the Boxing Kangaroo, the public of Vanity Fair found time to grin and chatter over the most intimate concerns of this reputed great man, who had so often lashed them with his scorn, and who was now held up to their inspection as a cantankerous old gentleman who was jealous of his contemporaries, was the cause of jealousy in his wife, and could be deprived of faith, hope, and charity by a barking dog, a crowing cock, an interviewer, or a bug. They gloated over the discovery. If this was greatness, why trouble to be great ? If this was virtue, they at all events could avoid it.

It may be said that the opinion of Vanity Fair is of no consequence. Certainly it is not of much consequence, unless it is triumphant ; but on this occasion for a while it triumphed. Many even of the very elect were shaken in their allegiance to their master. His reputation sank, the limits of his influence shrunk together, the ideals of life and work for which his name had stood were dimmed. There is no doubt that after the appearance of the biographical volumes, Carlyle's works were less read instead of more, and his teaching lost in authority instead of gaining. That is Froude's condemnation. It is quite possible to blame him to excess. There

was nothing mean or rancorous in his purpose.
His admiration of Carlyle was entirely genuine, and
so was his devotion to his master's memory. The
two last volumes of the "Life," whatever their
mistakes both in judgment and accuracy, will rank
with the finest pieces of biography in our language.
But in his determination not to be led away into
the common panegyric of biographers he went too
far on the other side. Instead of pleading, as most
writers plead, for the canonization of his hero, he
became unintentionally the "Advocatus Diaboli,"
and proved himself unhappily so successful on that
side of the case that Carlyle's name was excluded
from the roll, not only of the Saints, but of the
"Blessed." It was an error hardly pardonable ;
long ago it brought its revenges in the temporary
decline of Carlyle's reputation, and now new avengers
appear in the shape of Mr. Alexander Carlyle and
Sir James Crichton-Browne.

Their book is avowedly a counterblast. It is, as
they say, intended to refute Froude's errors, and
the refutation is often very shrill, especially when
Mr. Alexander Carlyle takes up the cry. Sir James
Crichton-Browne leads off with an introduction of
eighty-two scientific pages. Beyond proving that
all Froude's biographical works ought to have
been committed to the flames, his main object
is to show that Mrs. Carlyle, at the time when
she wrote the "Journal" upon which the chief

charge against her husband was founded, was passing through "a mild, but protracted attack of mental disturbance, which would be technically called on its psychical side climacteric melancholia, and on its physical side neurasthenia." He traces her hereditary tendency to nervous disorder. "Always highly neurotic," she was undermined, he thinks, by influenza, sleeplessness, and the morphia and other drugs she took for relief. Other signs of her "masked insanity," as he calls it, he finds in her reported interest in horrors about the time of the "Journal," and the crippling neuralgia which came upon her towards the end. In fact, the eminent man of science regards her as a mental patient, and attributes all her suspicions, her passionate misery, her lamentations, and sorrows, to the disordered condition of her own nerves.

No doubt this is all true in its way. There is a physical or medical side to all unhappiness, and sorrow, ever feeding on itself, moves in a vicious circle, the mind acting upon the body, and the body reacting upon the mind. But we who are not medical specialists cannot always be regarding character as a matter of pathology. If it came to that, we could imagine expressing Carlyle himself in terms of cerebral dyspepsia. But ordinary people have to take men and women pretty much as they find them in the rough. The nervous excitability, nervous weakness, and all the rest were part and parcel of

Mrs. Carlyle's brilliant and attractive personality. No doubt she paid the price, as all sensitive people pay it ; but that does not appear to us to prove that the unhappiness shown in her letters and "Journal" was otherwise causeless. Nor, indeed, did her own husband, when he came to read her words, regard them as the ravings of masked insanity. They filled him with sorrow and remorse, of which the expression may have been exaggerated, but the feeling was undoubtedly genuine.

The worst of combative writers like the editors of these volumes is that they are incapable of maintaining their hero's cause without tilting at other people now defenceless. In honour to Mrs. Carlyle, Froude spoilt one of the finest portraits in biography by overloading the shadows. And now, in honour to Carlyle, Sir James Crichton-Browne diagnoses Mrs. Carlyle as a semi-lunatic with superinduced neurasthenia, while Mr. Alexander Carlyle's notes would leave the unwary with the impression that she was a shrewish virago incapable either of tact or feeling.

Happily, we who are neither specialists in morbid conditions nor champions of a clan may take a calmer and wider view of things than the combatants. We find the greatest writer of his century and one of its most brilliant women bound by marriage to live together practically alone in the same small house for about forty years. In all the history of literary, philosophic, or poetic genius, from Socrates down to Byron and onward, we can for the moment think of only two instances of what is generally called a "happy marriage." No sane man or woman weds genius for fun, or even for comfort and what is usually meant by happiness ; and had Mrs. Carlyle done this, we should indeed have been obliged to concede her semi-lunacy. But she did no such thing. Being from the first a woman of shrewd judgment and profound intuition, as every line of her letters shows, she saw, like Goethe, the immense possibilities of future greatness and influence hidden in that unknown young Scotchman. She was attracted by that strong and humorous personality—an inspired prophet so full of laughter and compassion—who for the eighty-six years of his life never failed of that strange personal attraction. In later life she said she had married for fame, and had succeeded beyond her wildest hopes. Certainly she had succeeded, but it was not only fame for which she married. It was by admiration and by what for want of a better word we must call affection that she was drawn to Carlyle's side, where she stood on guard, as it were, till her life's end, loyally and not unhappily, considering the extreme difficulty of the situation.

As to that difficulty, she never had any fond illusions. "Live with you at Craigenputtock !" she wrote, when first the retirement to that lonely farm was proposed : "I would not live at

Craigenputtock with an Archangel ! " The touch of genius which she herself possessed only heightened the danger. Two people of brilliant and restless minds, both as sensitive as if they had no skin, both passionate in love and hatred, both nobly proud and nobly poor, both endowed with vehement eloquence and humorously aware of the consolations of rhetoric, both ailing in body and following for the most part an unhealthy indoor existence ; one the greatest teacher of his age but longing to be a man of action, the other the courted centre of a high intellectual group but longing for still further expression of her powers,—why, the wonder is, not that they lived at times unhappily, but that they lived at all ! The importance of the whole relationship, whether happy or not, has been absurdly exaggerated by people who like gossip, but care nothing about Carlyle's real work. But after rereading the letters of both to each other from start to finish, we are inclined to think that, even leaving genius out of the question, very few marriages that have lasted so long have really been as happy. Let any man or woman, whether of genius or not, who has been married, say, for thirty years, read those letters through, and say whether we are not right !

But leaving the dust and heat of controversy, let us turn with all gratitude to the new series of letters which the editors here give us. They are letters which Carlyle himself prepared and annotated for the memorials upon which he spent the best work of his regretful loneliness, but which Froude did not use in his selection. Of the much-discussed "Journal," which after all only covered a few months (October, 1855, to July, 1856) of a longish life, the second part is given entire, whilst the first part is altogether omitted, because the editor thinks Carlyle did not intend its publication. The letters are no better and no worse than those that the world has read before : they are exactly the same. They give us nothing new, except the new delight of more to read. Mrs. Carlyle has long ranked with Byron, Lamb, her husband, and one or two more among the best letter-writers in our language, and here we find again on every page the keen strokes of satire, the vivid description, the unfailing insight, and a kind of inspired good-sense which are her characteristics, and have no very obvious relationship to "masked insanity." Examples are plentiful, but we may take these two ; writing on a visit to her uncle in Scotland to John Carlyle, whose prose translation of the "Inferno" is well known, she says—

"We had been talking about you the other night, and then we had sunk silent, and I had betaken myself to walking to and fro in the room. Suddenly my uncle turned his head to me and said, shaking it gravely, 'He has made an awesome pluister o' *that* place !' 'Who? What place, uncle?' 'Whew ! the place ye'll maybe gang to if ye dinna tak' care !' I really believe he considers all those circles of *your* invention."

Or take the following picture of Mrs. Montagu in old age (1854)—

"I saw the 'Noble Lady' that night; and a strange tragic sight she was! sitting all alone in a low-ceilinged confined room at the top of Procter's house; a French bed in a corner, some relics of the grand Bedford Square drawing-room scattered about. Herself stately, artistic as ever; not a line of her figure, not a fold of her dress changed since we knew her first, twenty years ago and more! She made me sit on a low chair opposite to her, and began to speak of Edward Irving and long ago, as if it were last year—last month! There was something quite overpowering in the whole thing: the Pagan grandeur of the old woman, retired from the world, awaiting death, as erect and unyielding as ever, contrasted so strangely with the mean bedroom at the top of the house, and the uproar of company going on below. And the Past which she seemed to live and move in felt to gather round me, too, till I fairly laid my head on her lap and burst into tears! She stroked my hair very gently and said, 'I think, Jane, your manner never changes, any more than your hair, which is still black, I see.' 'But you, too, are not changed,' I said. 'You know,' she said, 'when I was still a young woman I dressed and felt like an old one, and so age has not told so much on me as on most others.'"

That is exactly the woman in her more serious moods, touched with irony. There is plenty of gaiety and playfulness too, and plenty of satire. "You would be a vast deal more amiable," old Sterling of the *Times* used to say to her, "if you were not so damnably clever." The cleverness was never exhausted, but, what appears to us far more

G

uncommon, her deep affection for her man of genius, in spite of all her unhappiness, intellectual jealousies, and griefs, was never exhausted either.   When all is said, and the Devil's Advocates on both sides have spoken their worst—when we consider how rare it is to live for sixty or eighty years without disaster, much more with an unfailing ideal and unflagging enthusiasm, we still maintain that, as marriages go, it would be difficult to imagine a marriage for either of the two that could have proved more successful in the highest sense of the word.

"*Forbeare !*"

ONE'S first thought in opening the "Nemesis of Froude" is, "Good Frend, for Jesus sake, forbeare !" That great old man, so magnificent in genius, so faithful to the noblest purposes, so full of scorn for the fashionable and inquisitive crowd; that great woman, so well matched with him in genius, so devoted to his honour, so brilliant herself in converse and letters, and so delicately sensitive to the horror of every vulgar and obtuse mind ;—why is it that people should go grubbing about for ever in the dust of their naked bones ? Their fate has made the very thought of biography detestable. Now, if ever, it is true that a new terror has been added to death. Henceforward, if men or women of genius be wise, they will cover up all traces of their earthly course before they go hence and are no more seen. Nothing will be spared. Their very bedrooms will be routed out, and for twenty or even forty years rival partisans will wrangle with the blind fury of religious sects over their scraps of dirty linen.

That this abomination should have befallen the Carlyles, of all people—that one party should be

howling "inconstant savage ! " over the man, whilst
another shrieks " neurotic maniac ! " over the woman
—is worse than the little ironies that beset everybody's life.   It is a genuine, though abhorrent,
tragedy, for the two human beings concerned were
of finer mould than ordinary mankind, and their
fate is just of the kind that they would have shrunk
from with the utmost loathing.   Well might the
spirit of each cry with Job, " The thing that I feared
has come upon me."

Over their poor graves in Haddington and Eccle-
fechan counterblast answers to counterblast, thunder
to thunder.   Hardly had the wild controversy
of twenty years ago fallen silent at last, hardly had
the true genius of Carlyle and his wife begun to
be recognized again for what it was, apart from
all the temporary and accidental stains that death
is wont to wipe off, when the editors of the present
volume must needs issue their " New Letters and
Memorials of Jane Welsh Carlyle," with an introduction and notes containing the most violent
accusations against Froude as Carlyle's biographer,
and what we must describe as a series of cruel
onslaughts upon the memory of Mrs. Carlyle
herself. Froude's son and daughter replied at
once in their father's defence by publishing a long
memorandum which he had himself left in their
hands for use if the occasion arose, called " My
Relations with Carlyle."   In this certain further

facts or theories were revealed that were supposed
to throw more light on Carlyle's character and the
causes of the reputed unhappiness of the marriage.
We did not consider the publication of any great
importance, for it brought little that was new to
those who had taken interest in these merely personal
and unessential matters of dispute, nor did we consider that the reputed unhappiness of the Carlyle
marriage was at all the most important part in the
lives of either of them.   As marriages go, especially
as the marriages of genius go, we even regard the
Carlyle marriage as rather peculiarly successful.   How
many women, after twenty years of marriage, write
to their husbands like this ?—

"I have grown to love you the longer, the more, till
now you are grown to be the whole universe, God, everything to me, but in proportion as I have got to know all
your importance to me I have been losing faith in my
importance to you."

Or take a letter written a few days before Mrs.
Carlyle's death : how many women after forty years
of marriage will thus write of a husband's triumph ?
Referring to public enthusiasm during the time of
the Edinburgh address, she says—

"I must repeat what I have said before—that the best
part of this success is the general feeling of personal good will
that pervades all they say and write about you.   Even
Punch cuddles you, and purrs over you, as if you were
his favourite son. . . . I tore it open (the telegram about

the address), and read, 'From John Tyndall.' (Oh, God bless John Tyndall in this world and the next)! 'A perfect triumph!'"

It appears to us ridiculous to make all this pother about the unhappiness of a marriage in which people continued to write to each other in that strain for forty years with hardly a break. When we remember the peculiar sensitiveness of both and their extraordinary powers of satire, denunciation, and general eloquence, their lot appears to us something above the lot of common mortality, and all this howling and shrieking falls meaningless upon the air.

However, Mr. Alexander Carlyle and Sir James Crichton-Browne do not agree with us. Instead of leaving Froude's posthumous defence alone, they reply with this " Nemesis of Froude," as though to put the full-stop to the career that began with the " Nemesis of Faith." Their object is the wholly laudable one of re-establishing Carlyle's character ; the means they choose seem to us more dubious. They abuse Froude as violently as they can, and they insinuate charges against Mrs. Carlyle as unpleasantly as they dare. In short, they follow up the methods of their first book, and with the same result. The reader at the end of it all remains unconvinced or indifferent because he feels that they are only partisans fighting their case with every weapon of violence and suspicion.

In their treatment of Mrs. Carlyle they are

perhaps not quite so venomous as in the former
volumes, and we suppose that Mr. Alexander Carlyle
especially has been held in check by the disgust
naturally aroused by his virulence against a dead
woman who would have been so well able to defend
herself had she been alive.   Yet the authors actually
speak of Mrs. Carlyle, of all people on earth, as " a
worldly little woman whose Godlessness was a rather
disenchanting element in her character."   They say
also, with less shadow of evidence than even Froude
had for his wildest theories, that she " became
involved in ambitious projects " in London, and
consequently—

"Like some of the fashionable women of the day, she
became more alive to the drawbacks than to the pleasures of
motherhood."

But for sanctimonious and insolent assumption
towards both the living and the dead, perhaps the
following sentence stands unrivalled in either of the
books—

"That Miss Welsh had shed whatever faith she once
possessed, and had developed some of the unlovely traits of
character which so often accompany that disrobement in a
woman, long before she fell under the influence of Carlyle,
is abundantly clear."

We need not point out the contemptible self-
righteousness that lies in a sentence like that.   This
is the sort of thing to which partisanship or personal

rancour may drive presumably honest and thoughtful natures.   We look and pass.

Beyond the pages on pages of abuse of Froude, unworthy sneers at his imaginary greed for money, and endless discussion of legal points with regard to the possession of Carlyle's papers—points which are of no earthly interest outside the family—the authors deal mainly with three subjects in the interminable Carlyle disputation.   They deny there was "anything in " the intimate friendship of Carlyle with Lady Ashburton.   Froude himself denied it, too, and obviously both sides are right for once.   But at the same time there can be no doubt that the intimacy caused Mrs. Carlyle much unhappiness, and we think it quite unnecessary for a specialist in lunacy to charge her with " masked insanity," " climacteric melancholia," and other sounding diseases on that account.   Again, they deny the charge that Carlyle "was one of those who ought never to have married," and they support the denial with many very beautiful and affectionate passages from the letters.   We prefer to give the only passage in which, as far as we know, Carlyle alludes to their childlessness himself—

" Her little bit of a first chair, its wee, wee arms, etc., visible to me in the closet at this moment, is still here and always was ; I have looked at it hundreds of times, from of *old* with many thoughts.   No daughter or son of *hers* was to sit there ; so it has been appointed us, my darling.   I have no *Book* thousandth-part so beautiful as *Thou ;* but these were our only 'children '—and in a true sense they were verily ours ; and will, perhaps, live some time in the world, after we are gone ;—and be of no damage to the poor brute chaos of a world, let us hope ! "

After sentences like that it seems to us mere trifling to discuss the " blue marks on the wrist," mentioned in a brief note of Mrs. Carlyle's diary, and to puzzle ourselves whether they came from violence, as Froude asserted, or from bugs, as the present authors playfully suggest. There are worse things to suffer and wonder over in the world than either bugs or fits of violence, and in neither case do those " blue marks " belong to what Carlyle loved to call the Eternities of the Universe. To those Eternities the genius of himself and his wife did in a very noble sense belong, and it is because books of this kind tend to distract us from the contemplation of those eternities and involve us in recriminations about the temporal and trivial, that we once more repeat our humble petition that this controversy should now be regarded as for ever closed, and, to the partisan of either side, we only pray again, " Good Frend, for Jesus sake, forbeare ! "

" *Carlyle's Letters* "

"CONTROVERSIAL topics have been avoided." How one rejoices over that little sentence in the preface to the " New Letters of Thomas Carlyle " ! After the " New Letters and Memorials of Jane Welsh Carlyle " in 1903, after the publication of Froude's " My Relations with Carlyle," and the present editors' answer in " The Nemesis of Froude," one was full of fears. It really seemed as if the miserable squabble of twenty years ago was never to be allowed to die, and the very bones of a man and woman of genius, singularly sensitive, proud, and retiring, were to be dangled for ever before the gaze of all the smart and vulgar people, the diners-out and the ghouls, who care nothing for genius beyond its weakness, and nothing for literature beyond its chatter. It seemed as though the great writer who exercised an un-equalled influence on the England of the nineteenth century, and the brilliant lady who gallantly fought at his side for forty years of poverty, struggle, and ultimate power, were to go down to time as figures in the trivial Punch and Judy show of unhappy marriage.

But now Mr. Alexander Carlyle, himself one of

the two worst offenders of late years, tells us we are
to have no more controversy, and let us only pray
him to keep his rule. In these two volumes it is
kept almost without a breach. The greater part of
the letters were selected by Professor Norton, in
continuation of his previous series that brought us
up, first to 1826, and then to 1836, where the
present series begins. And throughout we seem to
feel the touch of that sweet-tempered scholar and
deeply sympathetic man. Unhappily, he is now too
old to have edited the whole collection himself, but
Mr. Alexander Carlyle has contented himself this
time with the task of further selection and the
addition of a very few necessary notes. To call the
result " New Letters " is hardly exact, for a great
number of the letters had already been used, at least
in extract, for the second part of Froude's biography
—the " Life in London." But still, the editor may
fairly claim that they form a kind of " epistolary
autobiography," and if read in connection with the
earlier letters, the reminiscences, and Jane Welsh
Carlyle's " Letters and Memorials," they do present
us with an admirable picture, not only of a man of
extraordinary genius and character, but of the
thoughtful life of England during the greater part of
last century.

They begin when Carlyle was forty-one. " Sartor
Resartus," his most profound and imaginative work,
perhaps also the most influential upon thought, was

already behind him, and we find him upon what is the most dramatic scene in his masterpiece of historic drama—the book called " Varennes," in his " French Revolution." He has come to London—one cannot say " for good "—but for life. I think he sometimes recognized the grandeur—the filthy grandeur—of London, her sombre indifference, and heated stimulus to thought. Certainly he recognized the fatted beauty of her surrounding gardens and fields and heavy streams.

" Till this bout of riding," he writes to John Sterling in 1839, " I never knew what a most lovely country of its sort this London region is. Green, frondent, fertile, entirely subdued to man ; whatsoever all this in its utmost perfection can offer, without running water, rock or mountain, is there. The hectic dying beauty of some of the sun-glimpses I have come upon in my solitude are things to be enjoyed—in profound *silence*, you knave ! I am also greatly delighted with the country people, working on the roads, etc., down to the very children ; and rejoice to call such people my kindred."

He might rejoice ; provided they were not rich, fashionable, or professedly witty, he might, like his own Teufelsdröckh, have taken the whole of mankind to his bosom and kept it warm. But his heart was, none the less, in the Lowlands, where the little white farms gleam among the rocky hills, where burns of deep amber water run swirling down to the Solway, and the wind and shadows pass over the heather and boggy peat. There were the hard-

toiling, solemn, and quietly humorous people—
" grave livers "—who were indeed his kindred.
And there was the old woman of Scotsbrig farm,
who was his mother and truest friend. To her and
to his brothers—to Dr. Carlyle, the translator of
Dante, and Alexander Carlyle in Canada (who, as
he was dying in the backwoods, asked, " Is Tom
coming from Edinburgh the morn ? ")—to these
most of the letters are addressed, and to those
true homes of his spirit it was his unfailing consolation to return. Among the very few letters to
Carlyle included in these volumes are two or three
from his mother, showing in every line her profound
and serious nature. In one letter, after encouraging
him in his work over the French Revolution, and
reminding him where the mind must be stayed if it
would be kept in perfect peace, she adds—

" I think there are none that has so much cause of
thankfulness as I. We are all going on in the old way ;
but it has been such a year as I do not remember of for bad
weather. It has grown worse and worse. Nevertheless, it
is better than we deserve, for we are froward children, a
sinful generation."

And four years later she writes—

" MY DEAR SON,—
" I should have written long before now, but
always put off : I come so ill at it. Believe me it is
not for want of good will ; as you are so mindful of me,
so you are not long out of my mind. May God reward

you for your kindness. We are all in our usual way ; I am spinning on the big wheel ; it procures me sleep. Do you sleep well ? I often think on you when I am taking my smoke at bedtime. We may pray for one another. It is a great mercy we have free liberty. . . . I will be very warm through the winter, if I am spared, with my new dresses. May God clothe the givers with the robe of the Redeemer's righteousness."

In such passages we find, not the same form of faith, but the very mood in which her son habitually regarded the world. It is the mood of those who live very close to " the Eternities," and pay little heed to all that is trivial, transient, and untouched by the spirit. It is the mood of those whose Kingdom is within them, and whom neither powers, nor principalities, nor dominions, nor thrones, nor landlords, nor publishers, nor newspaper editors, nor the British public itself can ever harm or help. Such people, like the Happy Warrior, possess in themselves their own desire, and before we condemn Carlyle for his easy indifference or, perhaps, contempt towards so much that the society of his time regarded as marvellous and worshipful, we must remember from what a different world he had sprung, and how remote from social gossip were the things he had learnt to marvel at and worship. Till he was nearly forty he had lived, for the most part, in the solitudes of mountains and skies, or in small villages of earnest, labouring people, engaged in the primeval struggle of winning

their food and warmth from the earth. What satisfaction could he be expected to find among the
reputed wits and drawing-room writers of his day,
or among the social gatherings of people who had
never smelt a ploughed field, or known hunger or
cold or any of the ultimate realities of soul and
body ?   Let us recall those lines in the four
tremendous pages that he wrote on the death of
Edward Irving, the year before these letters open
(1835)—

"Irving was forty-two and some months old.   Scotland
sent him forth a Herculean man ; our mad Babylon wore
him and wasted him with all her engines ; and it took her
twelve years.   He sleeps with his fathers, in that loved
birthland ; Babylon with all its deafening insanity rages on ;
but to him henceforth innocuous, unheeded—for ever."

From a man of such temperament, and bred
among such solemn aspects of the universe, we
might fairly expect unusual judgments upon contemporary life and men.   There is no reason to
suppose the opinions of genius should be like
ordinary people's opinions.   And accordingly, much
as we may admire John Mill, for instance, and the
early Utilitarians who sixty years ago regarded
themselves, perhaps rightly, as in the very van of
progress, we must not be too much astonished at
passages like this—

"No sect in our day has made a wretcheder figure in
practice than the Bentham-Radical sect.   Nature abhors a

vacuum ; worthy old girl, she will not make a wretched, un-
sympathetic, scraggy Atheism and Egoism fruitful in her
world ; but answers to it : Enough, thou scraggy Atheism ;
go thy ways, wilt thou ! ''

It is violent, but who calls himself a Utilitarian now ?
Or where is that rather dry and unimaginative form
of denial which in those days passed as so scientific ?
As coming still closer to our line of thought, take
these sentences on the boasted " tolerance " of
advanced circles—

"On the whole, I take up my old love for the saints.
No class of person can be found in this country with as
much humanity in them ; nay, with as much tolerance as
the better sort of them have. The tolerance of others is
but doubt and indifference; touch the thing they do believe
in and value, their own self-conceit, and they are rattlesnakes
then ! ''

Again it is violent ; but who has not at some time
seen those rattlesnakes raise their heads, and heard
the tremulous threatening of their scales ?

It is too commonly thought that all his judgments on men and things were thus savage or
satiric. People forget, not only his extraordinary
generosity to any one in want and to any one
whom his influence could assist, but his long
friendships with men like John Sterling, John
Forster, Emerson, and Tyndall. Wherever he
found a genuine solidity of character and intellect,
he was singularly quick to welcome it, as in

the instances of Browning and Turgenieff shown
in these volumes. The testimony of Browning is
of peculiar value, for it was given after Carlyle's
death, at the time when detraction was doing its
vilest. The friendship began with some excellent
criticisms Carlyle wrote on " Sordello " and " Pippa
Passes." In 1885 Browning writes—

"The first of the letters was written, as you see, forty-
four years ago ; and the goodness and sympathy which began
so long ago continued unabated to the end of the writer's
life. I repaid them with just as enduring an affectionate
gratitude. It was not I who ventured to make the acquaintance or ask the correspondence of Carlyle : his love was
altogether a free gift, and how much it has enriched my
life, I shall hardly attempt to say."

These two volumes call up before us again the
picture of a true hero in the realm of letters. It is
a stern but inspiring picture, for the man lived with
the seriousness of one who never forgot the graves
under him or the stars above. Nothing diverted
him from his steady purpose. Till he was old
he remained poor. He thought himself fortunate
if he made £200 in a year. When he was far over
forty he speaks of his bitter thrift, and it was not till
then that he could write to his mother, " I have a
prospect of being able to live now with less misery
from the terror of want." Through all his years he
never flinched, or sought his ease, or doubted of his
message. The deep seriousness of his peasant stock,

the pity he had learnt for mankind among fields and cottage homes, the wild humour of the contrasts in the world—these things bore him on, and to the last of his working days he never paused in the labour he had set before him. " Rest ? Rest ? " cried his Teufelsdröckh ; " shall I not have all eternity to rest in ? "

The Poet Lovers

TO open a book like the "Letters of Robert Browning and Elizabeth Barrett Barrett," is like entering a room where lovers are. The first instinct is to withdraw silently before they are conscious of the intruder's presence. What right have we to be there? Of all letters written by the great, certainly these are the most obviously private. The idea of their publication to the world can never for a moment have entered the thoughts of the two poets at the time of writing. They are as secret and intimate as lovers' words of mouth. Heart is just speaking to heart, with not the smallest notion that some day the whole world would be admitted to overhear those confessions.

What, then, is the justification for the appearance of these volumes? The son of the two poets finds it in his father's implied wish—

"Ever since my mother's death these letters were kept by my father in a certain inlaid box, into which they exactly fitted, and where they have always rested, letter beside letter, each in its consecutive order, and numbered on the envelope by his own hand. My father destroyed all the rest of his

correspondence, and not long before his death he said, referring to these letters, 'There they are : do with them as you
please when I am dead and gone !' "

That sentence was no doubt an implied wish, an
implied command, especially when combined with
the destruction of all other correspondence. The
command entirely absolves Mr. Barrett Browning
from any possible charge of indiscretion or irreverence.
We do not see how he could have done anything
but obey. And yet, on the whole, though we have
read the book with an admiration for both the
writers, only increased by all they write, we should
still hesitate what answer to give, if it were possible
to hold back the publication, and we were called
upon to decide. It is hard to escape that feeling
of sacrilege—of breaking in upon the sanctities of
the dead. And besides, reticence is nearly always
good, and there are many things which should only
be spoken of to the world from behind a veil, such
as one of these poets habitually used in his works,
and the other often in hers.

On the other hand, if Mr. Barrett Browning had
thought it possible to raise a monument to his
parents which should increase, not perhaps their
fame, but our admiration for their personality, he
could have found no more fitting means than these
letters. They are published in their entirety, without the alteration or omission of a word, and
every letter has been preserved but one, which the

poet himself destroyed. They run through twenty-one months, and fill eleven hundred and fifty closely printed pages. There are not many people whose love-letters could be published so and yet never for a moment suggest either absurdity or half-heartedness.

We are not sure that the poets will rank with the great letter-writers of the world. Byron had surer wit and fresher spirit in a letter. The Carlyles wrote of wider interests, and they could flood the page with humour or engrave it with incisive phrase. Keats could interpenetrate every word with a peculiar strength and beauty of passion. The Brownings had other qualities, and their style was not at its very best in letter-writing, good though it was. Circumstances also made their subjects very limited—kept almost within the bounds of books and themselves. Yet we may say that even as letters these volumes will rank high, while we believe they are unique as a record of two kindred souls meeting, neither too late nor too soon, but in the fulness of time, when their rare comradeship could develop in both a power surpassing even the promise of their previous work, and could lead them forward to a happiness of union seldom realized. About once in three ages, says Montaigne, in speaking of his friendship with Etienne, may such a thing occur, and there is no reason to suppose that fate brings about the perfect union of man and woman more

frequently. But here in this collection of old leaves
is an unequalled monument of so rare a consummation. As such the world will welcome it ; for
though misery gives gossip more to talk about, it
is joy that leaves the imperishable and uplifting
memory. In their dignity as in tenderness the
letters are worthy of the two noble lives which here
combine, and perhaps the strangest part of it all is
that we are sure there is not a word which either
would erase if now they could re-read what they
wrote then.

The first letter is dated January 10, 1845, and
is from Browning, expressing his admiration for
Miss Barrett's poems, which had been first
collected in the previous year. Browning was now
thirty-three, and was bringing out the " Bells and
Pomegranates " in cheap parts. Extraordinary as
his performance had already been, his power had
hardly yet reached maturity, and he had still about
twenty years before it showed a sign of waning.
Elizabeth Barrett was about three years older,
and under the influences of that year her genius
undoubtedly attained to its full height. For six
years, since the shock of her favourite brother's
sudden death, she had lived an invalid existence,
shut up in a darkened room. The illness was due
in part to an over-sensitive mind, and her way
of life only increased it, throwing her in upon
herself, and confining her interests mainly to books

and one or two sympathetic friends. From Browning's first letter we learn that they nearly met some years earlier, and we may wonder whether her imprisonment would not have been shorter had she then encountered that vigorous and open-air nature.

" Do you know I was once not very far from seeing you —really seeing you? Mr. Kenyon said to me one morning, 'Would you like to see Miss Barrett?' then he went to announce me—then he returned . . . you were too unwell, and now it is years ago, and I feel as at some untoward passage in my travels, as if I had been close, so close, to some world's wonder in chapel or crypt, only a screen to push and I might have entered, but there was some slight, so it now seems, slight and just sufficient bar to admission, and the half-opened door shut, and I went home my thousands of miles, and the sight was never to be ? "

It is a characteristic sentence, not only for its rapid and haphazard manner and the queer punctuation (which both writers use), of dots, dashes, and question-marks, but more still for the headlong fervour with which the poet, writing to an unknown lady, speaks from his heart at once, setting aside all conventional constraints and ceremonies. She answers next day, more quietly, perhaps, but with the same freedom and intimacy. She asks for a sentence or two of general observation and advice, is half-glad he did not come to her crypt for fear he might have been chilled, and concludes—

" While I live to follow this divine art of poetry, in proportion to my love for it, and my devotion to it, I must

be a devout admirer and student of your works.   This is in
my heart to say to you—and I say it."

She was answered at once, and in her second
letter she drops a hint to which perhaps we owe
a manifest change in the subsequent method of
Browning's art—

"You have an immense grasp in art ; and no one at all
accustomed to consider the usual forms of it, can help
regarding with reverence and gladness the gradual expansion
of your powers.   Then you are 'masculine' to the height
—and I, as a woman, have studied some of your gestures of
language and intonation wistfully, as a thing beyond me far !
and the more admirable for being beyond. . . . A great
dramatic power may develop itself otherwise than in the
formal drama ; and I have been guilty of wishing before this
hour that you would give the public a poem unassociated
directly or indirectly with the stage, for a trial on the
popular heart.   I reverence the drama, but——"

So the correspondence goes rapidly forward, week
by week.   On the whole, we think she was a shade
the better letter-writer of the two, though their style
in letters as in verse has a similarity.   At first she
is a little formal and inevitably bookish.   But she is
always intelligible, and that is the first thing in a
letter, whereas Browning, especially in these earlier
messages, is sometimes overtaken by his " Sordello "
style ; once even her sympathetic eyes can decipher
no meaning, and queer sentences like the following
are not uncommon :—

"When I spoke of you knowing little of me, one of the senses in which I meant so was this—that I would not well vowel-point my common place letters and syllables with a masoretic *other* sound and sense, make my ' dear ' something intenser than ' dears ' in ordinary, and 'yours ever' a thought more significant than the run of its like."

There are also glimpses of the outside world— glimpses of people he meets, of Tennyson, Thackeray, and, above all, Carlyle, who is brought before us in the prime of his generous powers, uncmbittered still.

"I know Carlyle and love him—know him so well that I would have told you he had shaken that great head of his at ' singing,' so thoroughly does he love and live by it.

"When I last saw him, a fortnight ago, he turned, from I don't know what other talk, quite abruptly on me with, ' Did you never try to write a song ? Of all things in the world *that* I should be proudest to do.' Then came his definition of a song—then, with an appealing look to Mrs. C., ' I always say that some day, *in spite of nature and my stars*, I shall burst into a song.' . . . And just before I left England, six months ago, did not I hear him croon, if not certainly sing, ' Charlie is my darling' (' my *darling*' with an adoring emphasis), and then he stood back, as it were, from the song, to look at it better, and said, ' How must that notion of ideal wondrous perfection have impressed itself in this old Jacobite's " Young Cavalier" (*Chevalier*, no doubt, Carlyle said really), ' when I, who care nothing about such a rag of a man, cannot but feel as he felt, in speaking his words after him ! ' After saying which, he would be sure to counsel everybody to get their heads clear of singing ! "

On Browning's side, at all events, the expression of each letter becomes warmer. Then the thought of a possible visit is repeated. She shrinks from seeing him—from his seeing her, and it is easy to sympathize with her hesitation. At last she allowed him to come to Wimpole Street (the address of all her letters, as New Cross was of his). It was four months after the correspondence began ; he had loved her already with a love before first sight, and two days after he evidently wrote to tell her so. That was the letter which he destroyed after she had sent it back with a dignified insistence that there must never be a word of such things again.

"You have said some intemperate things, . . . fancies which you will not say over again, nor unsay, but forget at once and for ever having said at all ; and which (so) will die out between you and me alone, like a misprint between you and the printer. And this you will do for my sake, who am your friend (and you have none truer)—and this I ask because it is a condition necessary to our future liberty of intercourse. You remember—surely you do—that I am in the most exceptional of positions, and that, just because of it, I am able to receive you as I did on Tuesday. . . . Now, if there should be one word of answer attempted to this, or of reference, I must not—I will not—see you again, and you will justify me later in your heart."

After "last words" on both sides, the outburst of something more than friendship, or at least the mention of it, was resolutely repressed. They write of books again, and other things ; of old Wordsworth's presentation at Court among them.

"And now we shall hear of 'Luria,' shall we not?" she writes, "and much besides. And Miss Mitford has sent me the most highly comical of letters to read, addressed to her by 'R. B. Haydon, historical painter,' which has made me quite laugh, and would make you, expressing his righteous indignation at the 'great fact' and gross impropriety of any man who has 'thoughts too deep for tears' agreeing to wear a bag-wig."

Alas! that great fact is far enough from making us laugh; and so is the further information that the bag-wig and other nonsensical haberdashery were lent by Rogers, and the sword by David Wilkie, and that "the Laureate, so equipped, fell down on both knees in the superfluity cf etiquette, and had to be picked up by two lords-in-waiting." And yet there are some people who are anxious to be called Laureate —perhaps as their only way to be called poet as well.

But it was in vain that the lovers talked so resolutely of art and gossip, or of this and that. The old appeal was calling them, and in spite of all her determinations, it gave her no rest. Her persistence came from more than womanly caution and reserve. Prostrate and buried for years, she had ceased to believe that love would ever come. The thing might all be a passing fancy, or, even if real, it would only clog and hinder the poet lover on his way. She was terrified of "generosity." Her helplessness might well arouse in a generous nature something that worked like love, and was not.

Then there was her home life, under a father who loved her in his own savage way, but was overbearing in his tyranny almost to insanity. He was a slightly exaggerated type of the British family despot, whom nature made to match the British matron. His main rule in life was always to act exactly contrary to the wishes of those he loved. There were, for instance, endless debates and plans about a proposed visit to Italy, when first she began to recover, and could go for an occasional drive, or walk a few steps. The question kept every one in great anxiety for weeks, till at last, finding her heart was set on going, he refused altogether. There were reasons enough for her hesitation. But at the end of August her lover goes back to his theme again—

"I believe in *you* absolutely, utterly—I believe that when you bade me that time be silent—that such was your bidding, and I was silent—dare I say I think you did not know at that time the power I have over myself, that I could sit and speak and listen as I have done since? Let me say now—this only once—that I loved you from my soul, and gave you my life, so much of it as you would take, and all that is *done*, not to be altered now; it was, in the nature of the proceeding, wholly independent of any return on your part."

Her answer is one long struggle between tenderness and resolution.

"I asked for silence, but *also* and chiefly for the putting away of . . . You know very well what I asked for. And this was sincerely done, I attest to you. You wrote once to me—oh, long before May and the day we met—that you 'had been so happy, you should be now justified to yourself in taking any step most hazardous to the happiness of your life,' but if you were justified could *I* be, therefore, justified in abetting such a step ? . . . I thought, too, at first, that the feeling on your part was a mere generous impulse, likely to expend itself in a week perhaps. . . . Your life ! if you gave it to me and I put my whole heart into it, what should I put but anxiety and more sadness than you were born to ? What could I give you which it would not be ungenerous to give ? Therefore we must leave this subject, and I must trust you to leave it without one word more."

He really did leave it fairly faithfully for just a fortnight. Then he brought his answer to bear— the irrefutable lover's answers—and even descended to questions of livelihood—

" For my own future way in the world I have always refused to care—any one who can live a couple of years and more on bread and potatoes, as I did once on a time, and who prefers a blouse and a blue shirt (such as I now write in) to all manner of dress and gentlemanly appointment, and who can if necessary groom a horse not so badly, or, at all events, would rather do it all day long than succeed Mr. Fitzroy Kelly in the Solicitor-Generalship—such an one need not very much concern himself beyond considering the lilies how they grow. But now I see you near this life, all changes—and at a word I will do all that ought to be done, and let ' all my powers find sweet employ,' as Dr. Watts sings, in getting whatever is to be got—not very much, surely."

She answers with the array of her insuperable

reasons, and after them she, too, descends to worldly matters—

"I might certainly tell you that my own father, if he knew that you had written to me *so*, and that I had answered you—*so*, even, would not forgive me at the end of ten years —and this from none of the causes mentioned by me here, and in no disrespect to your name and your position, . . . though he does not over-value poetry even in his daughter, and is apt to take the world's measure of the means of life, . . . but for the singular reason that he never does tolerate in his family (sons or daughters) the development of one class of feelings."

As to money, she adds that she could not be very poor, if she wished, with three or four hundred a year, of which no living will could dispossess her. "And is not the chief good of money the being free from the need of thinking of it?" So the contest between love and duty went on, love slowly winning point by point, for, in fact, he held the citadel already, and was himself the higher duty besides, if we may call him by so chilly a word. At last, near the end of September, the struggle was over, or at least the victory was inevitable. She writes—

"And now listen to me in turn. You have touched me more profoundly than I thought even you could have touched me—my heart was full when you came here to-day. Henceforward I am yours for everything, but to do you harm . . . a promise goes to you that none, except God and your will, shall interpose between you and me. . . . I mean that if He should free me within a moderate time from the trailing chain of this weakness, I will then be to you whatever at that hour you shall choose, . . . whether friend or more than friend . . . a friend to the last in any case. So it rests with God and with you—only, in the meanwhile you are most absolutely free."

So came about the crisis and consummation of their lives. Then it was that she might write, in perhaps the greatest lines even among her sonnets—

> "Straightway I was 'ware
> So weeping, how a mystic Shape did move
> Behind me, and drew me backward by the hair;
> And a voice said in mastery, while I strove—
> 'Guess now who holds thee?' 'Death,' I said. But, there,
> The silver answer rang : 'Not Death, but Love.'"

Other lovers had come to her—one was rather a trouble still—but here was a thing which surpassed thought and expectation. An uncle had once said to her, "Do you beware of ever loving ! If you do, you will not do it by half : it will be for life and death." Now it was for life and death. As she writes—

"Believe it of me, dear dearest, that I, who am as clearsighted as other women . . . and not more humble (as to the approaches of common men), was quite resolutely blind when you came—I could not understand the possibility of *that*. It was too much—too surpassing. And so it will seem to the end. The astonishment, I mean, will not cease to be. It is my own especial fairy-tale."

The one blot on it all was the supposed necessity

for concealment.   Her terror of her father would be
almost inconceivable, one may hope, to most women
now.   No doubt it was partly due to her sepulchred
life, her extreme weakness and shattered nerve.   She
was thirty-seven, she had sufficient property of her
own, she was among the most celebrated women in
England.   Yet she trembled at the thought of her
father's rage, and concealed one of the deepest and
happiest affections in history for one of the noblest
of the century's poets, as though it had been a base
intrigue with a clown.   She could not hide it from
her sisters, but almost every day came the terror
lest some friend should see it in her eyes and betray
her.   Of course, they did see it, but, to their credit,
they held their peace.   It was in vain that Browning
urged her to make no secrets, or, at all events, to
resign her property and come with him at once.
For him, in spite of happiness, it was an almost
intolerable time.   He wrote that he could not endure
another year of it.   His visits were secret, and had
to be carefully arranged, but even then the father
sometimes heard of them, or he suspected some
reserve in his daughter's manner, and called her
"mumpish."   It was a period almost of degradation.
We cannot doubt that any open defiance would have
been better.   Yet she absolutely refused to allow it.
She felt that the cruel words of abuse would kill her.
She knew that separation from her lover would then
be complete, that letters would be stopped, and

perhaps she even feared personal violence. If all were known, she writes, Browning might save himself the trouble of coming upstairs, for she would be thrown to him out of the window on to the railings below.

It went on for a year, and they bore it as best they could, sustained, for one thing, by their terror at the common married state as illustrated in their acquaintance. They strove to continue their creative work also, and assumed an interest in daily life. She writes of her joy in treading on grass again, her interest in driving to see the railway train come in on the Western line, or to visit the country lanes towards Hampstead. They repeat some stories and humorous scenes which came in their way.

"You said" (she writes) "that you had heard only six words from Mr. Reade—but that they were characteristic. Some one was talking before him and you of the illness of Anacreon Moore. 'He is very ill,' said the some one. '*But he is no poet,*' said Mr. Reade. Isn't it a good story? Mr. Kenyon called it exquisite."

It is exquisite, but the best of stories is poor consolation to a lover. Besides, the usual virulent gossip was whispering other stories about previous affections and even previous marriages. His answer is fine—

"As to the 'Yorkshire Tragedy,' I hold myself rather aggrieved by it—they used to get up better stories of Lord Byron—and even I told you, anticipatingly, that I caused

I

that first wife of mine to drown and hang herself—whereas now, it turns out she did neither, but bade me do both . . . nay, was not my wife after all ! "

At last arrangements were made for the escape. Certainly no fairy prince ever had more trouble in rescuing the enchanted princess from an ogre's castle. Against her will, he insisted on going through the marriage formula before they went. They met one September morning in Marylebone Church, and after the service she returned at once to her prison, trembling at every breath.   An hour afterwards he writes—

"Words can never tell you—form them, transform them any way—how perfectly dear you are to me—perfectly dear to my heart and soul. I look back, and in every point, every word and gesture, every letter, every *silence*—you have been entirely perfect to me. I would not change one word, one look."

To which she answers—

"I sit as in a dream, when left to myself. I cannot believe or understand. Oh! but in all this difficult, embarrassing, and painful situation, I look over the palms to Troy—I feel happy and exulting to belong to you, past every opposition, out of sight of every will of man—none can put us asunder, now, at least. I have a right now openly to love you, and to hear other people call it a *duty* when I do,—knowing that if it were a sin, it would be done equally."

A week after, she and her maid sent their little

baggage to a station, walked out of the giant's cave without a word to any human soul, and when the giant came ravening back in the evening, he found, poor man, that his dearly loved daughter had fled and was gone for ever. It is indeed "a lesson for fathers," and perhaps a lesson for daughters too. As is well known, he refused ever to see her again, and all her letters were afterwards returned to her unopened. On the evening before the flight, she writes to Browning—

"I will not write more—I cannot. By to-morrow at this time I shall have *you* only, to love me—my beloved ! you *only!* As if one said *God only !* . . . Is this my last letter to you, ever dearest ? Oh—if I loved you less . . . a little, little less. Why, I should tell you our marriage was invalid, or ought to be. . . . It is dreadful . . . dreadful . . . to have to give pain here by a voluntary act—for the first time in my life."

It *was* her last letter to him. For fifteen years they were never separated, and then it was only death that came.

The Poet of Grotesque

TO those who came to the study of Browning during the last ten years of the poet's life, who sought or gave illumination, perhaps, in the Browning Society, and with the glorious zeal of apostolic youth discovered meanings and systems of which the poet himself never dreamed, it might appear impossible to say anything fresh upon a subject that has been so closely investigated and so thickly enveloped in dissertation. Yet Mr. Chesterton's book upon Browning gives us, above all things, a sense of freshness. The author appears to be ready to say something fresh at a moment's notice about any subject in the universe. If he does not give us a paradox, he states the obvious with such a convincing assurance of its novelty and value that we feel it is no less strange than one of his paradoxes, and no less true. To him the meanest 'bus that goes can give thoughts that do often lie too deep for laughter. The Prayer-book directs brides not to be afraid with any amazement; Mr. Chesterton is certainly not afraid, but he goes about the world in a perpetual state of astonishment and amaze.

It is a most enviable condition, for there is nothing depressing or satiric in his wonder. It is as though, in contemplating oceans, and mountains, and sewage, and the motor-car, he gave them all his blessing because he sees they are all very good. It may, of course, be possible to overdo this boisterous optimism. It would certainly be possible to pour out volumes of parody upon it. Take any ordinary transaction, for instance, and tell it in his manner—

" The young man carrying his evening dress and pulling off his gloves is quite as elemental a figure as any anchorite, quite as incomprehensible, and indeed quite as alarming. Rubbing a wax vesta upon his breeches, he kindles as by a miracle the Promethean spark. He looks round upon the *débris* of human souls—old dresses, the very emblems of true poetry, old rings in which the artificial glass recalls the sparkle of Brazilian mines, old watches to which time had become one with eternity, old clarionets whose last thin wail is now speeding through undulating ether at many thousand miles a second in the direction of our nearest neighbour in the Milky Way. Full of the passion of elemental tears, the young man, himself so justly described as a spark, hands his parcel over the counter to the merciless mercy of the pawnbroker, that astounding representative of human confidence and wealth."

But, indeed, there is little call to parody Mr. Chesterton. Like other writers whom he mentions in this book, he parodies himself—

" If he looked at a porcelain vase or an old hat, a cabbage, or a puppy at play, each began to be bewitched with the spell of a kind of fairyland of philosophers ; the vase, like the jar in the 'Arabian Nights,' to send up a smoke of thoughts and shapes ; the hat to produce souls, as a conjurer's hat produces rabbits ; the cabbage to swell and overshadow the earth, like the Tree of Knowledge ; and the puppy to go off at a scamper along the road to the end of the world."

It is partly true of Browning, of whom it is said, but of Mr. Chesterton it is true from first to last. No matter. It is just because of this schoolboy freshness, this rush of spirits like a Newfoundland dog's, and these bright glimpses of eternity in every gutter, that Mr. Chesterton was exactly the right man for Mr. John Morley to choose for the volume on Browning in his series.

On the biographical side the author wisely takes little account of those facts of which most biographies are made up — the unilluminating facts of birth, death, marriage, travels, money, and acquaintance-ship. He seeks only after two things, the nature of the poet's character and the nature of his art, and he begins with the typical paradox—

" Browning's work has the mystery which belongs to the complex ; his life the much greater mystery which belongs to the simple. He was clever enough to understand his own poetry ; and if he understood it, we can understand it. But he was also entirely unconscious and impulsive, and he was never clever enough to understand his own character ; consequently we may be excused if that part of him which was hidden from him is partly hidden from us."

The paradox is not quite true. We may say

that no man understands his own character, and it is
not important that he should. But it is important
that his biographer should, and in that Mr. Chesterton
shows his highest skill. As to his judgments upon
Browning's art there may well be two opinions,
though in the main we agree with him, but we think
there can be no question as to the brilliance and
truth with which he has conceived the poet's
character as a man. The idea which is formed
from reading the book as a whole is, indeed, a
masterly portrait, by far the finest interpretation
we have ever read of the man as he lived and
moved. How exactly, for instance, does the following passage call up the attractive but carefully dressed
and rather conventional gentleman of the healthy
middle classes, whom I at one time used to watch
Monday after Monday at the Popular Concerts !—

"He took pleasure beyond all question in himself ; in
the strictest sense of the word he enjoyed himself. But his
conception of himself was never that of the intellectual. He
conceived himself rather as a sanguine and strenuous man, a
great fighter. . . . His faults, a certain occasional fierceness
and grossness, were the faults that are counted as virtues
among navvies and sailors and most primitive men. His
virtues, boyishness, and absolute fidelity, and a love of plain
words and things, are the virtues which are counted as vices
among the æsthetic prigs who pay him the greatest honour.
. . . He was not vain of being an extraordinary man. He
was only somewhat excessively vain of being an ordinary
one."

We object to the cheap and obsolete abuse of
" æsthetic prigs," because, for one thing, Browning
was never a god of the " æsthetic " movement, for
obvious reasons ; but the rest is singularly just
and penetrating. So, again, when speaking of the
peculiar affection with which Browning was regarded
by such men as Carlyle and Landor, who were by no
means easy to please, Mr. Chesterton truly says—

"When a man is loved by other men of his own
intellectual stature and of a wholly different type and order
or eminence, we may be certain that there was something
genuine about him, and something far more important than
anything intellectual. Men do not like another man because
he is a genius, least of all when they happen to be geniuses
themselves."

Equally fine is what the author says about
Browning's "ardent and headlong conventionality,"
his splendid "barbarism," his optimism springing,
not from opinion, but from life, and his artless love
of society, like that of a citizen of the New Jerusalem
who desired with perfect sanity and simplicity to
be also a citizen of Mayfair. The treatment of the
Browning marriage is admirable too, and one may
especially notice the skilful analysis which shows
that, in spite of his one great breach of conventions,
Browning was not the sort of man that makes a
revolutionist, or cries out against all the rest of the
world because on one point he has gone his own
way. As a piece of portraiture the book is notably
successful.

The criticism of the poet's work is not quite so satisfactory, though, as we have said, we agree with the judgments in the main. The chief error, we think, is the very proper and enviable error of indiscriminate admiration. Mr. Chesterton hardly says enough upon the extraordinary beauty of much of the earlier work, such as "Sordello," but when "Pippa" is passed, he has hardly anything but the highest praise for all the succeeding works, with the one exception of "Pacchiarotto." We love an admiring critic, but still he ought to show some difference between such things as "The Worst of It," or "The Bishop Ordering his Tomb," and such things as "Fifine" or the "Parleyings." (And, by the way, Mr. Chesterton makes the careless mistake of saying the "Parleyings" was the last book published during the poet's lifetime, whereas he lived to hear of the great reception given to "Asolando," and said, "This is all very gratifying," soon before he died.) From the point of view, not of immortality, which is absurd, but of a century or so, we firmly believe that the one class will be regarded as work of true excellence, and the other as merely temporary or stillborn stuff. Even such really noble conceptions as "The Ring and the Book" will be known only to an occasional student or professor, though Mr. Chesterton gives a whole chapter to it. The real Browning will float down the stream of time on the little raft made of the two volumes of his own selections, and one by one the other things in the grand series of his works must inevitably sink of their own weight.   It is bitter to say this, for we admire them all, and have gained much from them all ; but we have not the slightest doubt that it is true, however bitter.

We do not blame Mr. Chesterton for never stopping to discuss any particular difficulty, though we should much like his opinion on certain passages, such as the central pause in " Sordello," the poem of " Easter Day," and such a line as that on the " certain hell-deep instincts " in " Blougram."   But we think his proportion is sometimes astray, as when he discusses " Mr. Sludge," a fine and very characteristic work, but hardly requiring nine pages out of the twenty-six, which is all the author leaves himself for the very considerable subject of " The Philosophy of Browning."   We would not, however, take leave of so inspiriting and in the literal sense edifying a book as this with any word of blame. Nearly everything that Mr. Chesterton says upon this great poet of the grotesque, this realist of passion, this observer so alive to the enormous importance of small things, is a delight to read, and a fine theme for the best kind of discussion, even where agreement does not follow at once. We feel that if Browning had been given his own choice, this is the kind of biographer and critic he would have taken for himself.

The Master of Comedy

AT last, in Mr. Benjamin Rogers's translations of Aristophanes, we are likely to get an edition worthy of the supreme comedian. With Aristophanic inconsequence, the fifth volume is the first to be born, but if the rest of the family are like it, all true humorists, whether they are Greek scholars or not, will assuredly rejoice. For here we have a carefully collated text, scholarly notes of explanation, introductions on the history of the plays, their subjects and metres, and, above all, we have an admirable English translation, reproducing for English readers the true spirit of the Athenian in all its moods—the moods of the satirist, the dreamer, the statesman, the jester, the patriot, the candlestick-maker, the monthly nurse, the scavenger, the fried-fish wife, and the decadent poet.

Mr. Rogers may almost be said to be doing for Aristophanes what Jowett did for Plato. No scholar could have a higher aim or finer reward. Like Jowett, he has lived himself into his subject, and seems to speak with the mouth of his master. Perhaps he had better have left out all protest upon the dramatist's frank indecency. The genuinely

humorous mind is often indecent, and certainly there
has been no human being so closely akin to Aristophanes as Rabelais. We must take such men as
they come, and be thankful. But, after all, Mr.
Rogers does not insist much upon the matter, and
his translations, though careful of offence, are never
squeamish. They run with the rollicking tolerance,
the outspoken acceptance of all things human, that
marks the humorous spirit.

He gives us here, as a first instalment, the
" Frogs " and the " Ecclesiazusæ." They are both
fine specimens of the master, and both are singularly
modern in their interest. They are peculiarly
parallel in another respect too ; into both long
episodes appear to have been spatch-cocked (thanks
to General Buller for the word !) just before their
performance — episodes apparently suggested by
striking literary events, the death of Euripides and
the appearance of Plato's " Republic."

Of the " Frogs " and its significance Browning
has told us the story in " Aristophanes' Apology,"
with learning and true insight, though with a natural
prejudice on the side of " Euripides the human."
But Browning's poem is long and not very easy.
For the moment, an English reader might perhaps
grasp the interest of the play to the audience which
heard it first, if he imagined Ibsen had been dead
four months and Shakespeare only fifty years. Let
us also suppose, if we can, that the scene in

Hades, as performed by Mr. Tree's company in
"Ulysses," did not represent a series of funny peep-
shows at which no baby could shudder, but the
actual realm of the dead into which all the spectators
firmly believe they will themselves one day pass ;
at least, if they are decently religious and respectable
people, they are bound to believe it. Let us further
suppose that our city is at a crisis of its fate compared to which the black week of Colenso was nothing
in blackness. She is tottering on the edge of a doom
worse than befell Paris when the Prussians poured
through her gates. War has been lasting twenty-
two years. It has been a war of endless miscalcu-
lations ; the leaders of the State have proved
themselves incapable either of war or peace, and the
party of reform spends all its time in mutual recriminations and suspicions.

At such a moment the master of burlesque shows
us the god of the stage trudging off with his servant,
a donkey, and a bundle of wraps, to Hades. In his
despair he is going to bring back one of the dead to
guide the distracted State. Ibsen, that is to say
Euripides, is just the man, he thinks. And there,
of course, we come upon an idea so Greek, so
entirely un-English, that we can hardly follow the
parallel. A poet is the last man we should make
Prime Minister. The French, with their superb
worship of genius in every form—their worship of
Victor Hugo, for instance, as a political guide—

could follow the Greek mind easily. But in our case, when our imagined poet went on to prove by a contest of criticism in Hades, that Shakespeare and not Ibsen was really the man to choose as saviour of society, we should have to interpret the two poets at once into types of mind and morality. And that, of course, was the old comedian's hidden intention too. In Æschylus, who stood to him as Shakespeare stands to us, he found the type of man who made Athens great in the spacious days when the united citizens overthrew the Persian armada—the type of man that Æschylus describes in Mr. Rogers's admirable rendering—

" For just consider what style of man he received from me, great six-foot high
    Heroical souls who never would blench from a townsman's duties in peace or war ;
    Not idle loafers, or low buffoons, or rascally scamps such as now they are.
    But men who were breathing spears and helms, and the snow-white plume in its crested pride,
    The greave, and the dart, and the warrior's heart in its seven-fold casing of tough bull-hide."

Such was the hero of the good old times when the country was at her best. But in Euripides (let us again call him the Ibsen of the time) the patriot-satirist discovers only the signs of party spirit, the sophistical mind, hair-splitting casuistry, effeminate chatter, godlessness, decadence, and the problem play. The criticism has all the necessary unfairness of burlesque. From this distance, we accept both the poets, and can only marvel that one little city in one generation gave us two such men, and so many more. But burlesque though the play is, we must remember that it won the rare distinction of being twice crowned by the Athenian people, and it was crowned, not for its humour or satire, but for its seriousness—the patriotic wisdom with which it urged all citizens to forget the animosities of the moment and unite for their country's salvation.

Frogs do not twitter and sing in England as they do in the Greek valleys, so that on our stage it would be difficult to get an equivalent to the ghostly creatures which chant in the marshes beside the Styx. Nor could we find anything really parallel to the Mystics or Initiated who act as Chorus in the play ; though perhaps Mrs. Besant and the Esoteric Buddhists might do at a pinch, or we could call in the more devout of the Psychical Researchers !

For the " Ecclesiazusæ," or " Women in Parliament "—the third of the poet's plays on women— there would be no trouble at all in finding the modern counterparts, for the play turns on the two questions of Woman and Utopia, and those never change. It came out twelve years later than the " Frogs," but the dramatist is still labouring for the redemption of the State, and he still seeks it by a kind of burlesque Conservatism.

Who are the true Conservatives ? Obviously,
women. From age to age they go on dyeing their
wool, and baking their bread, and cooking their
onions, and combing their hair, and smacking
their children, and abusing their husbands, just as
they have always done. In a scene of unequalled
comedy we are shown the wives of Athens assembled
in Parliament, dressed in their husbands' clothes.
They take over the management of the State, and
suddenly, instead of Toryism, they enact a revolution at which the wildest anarchist would gasp. No
doubt, as Mr. Rogers says, the poet is having his
fun with the Platonic Republic, but there is no need
to suppose the whole conception of the play is
deliberately altered. Woman as the revolutionary
Tory is equally true to nature and delightful to
comedy. And so the Conservative women at once
abolish all private property, even in themselves ; "all
private establishments are fused into one ;" they
abolish want and poverty by law ; they abolish law ;
and finally, at the State's expense, they give a
gorgeous love-feast to which they kindly invite their
husbands, and we leave them all revelling upon the
gloriously Gargantuan compound—

" Plattero—filleto—mulleto—turboto—Cranio—morselo
—pickelo—acido—Silphio—honeyo—pouredonthe—topothe
—Ouzelo—throstleo— cushato — culvero— Cutleto — roast-
ingo— marrowo — dippero— Leveret — syrupo— gibleto —
wings ! "

Æschylus at Stratford, 1904

IT was the Vigil of St. George, and Stratford was busy preparing for the Shakespeare Festival of the morrow. All day long it had rained, and the wind had driven the lambs under the hedges and shaken the pear-blossom in the cottage gardens. But at evening the sky cleared, and across the low-lying "heart of England," with its quiet streams, one could see again the round hills that lead up to Cotswold, and far away the blue outline of Malvern, with promise of Wales. In exact harmony with the scene, we had for the last two nights been witnessing the *Winter's Tale* and the *Merry Wives*, breathing the very soul of English comedy and farce ; and we had hardly done wondering whether Mr. Benson's "Dr. Caius," or Mr. Weir's "Falstaff" came nearer to the laughter-loving spirit of our race, when suddenly we heard an alien and deeper note upon the air.

In a moment we were transferred to Athens in the first wonder of her glory, and in place of the daisy-pied meadows of the Avon we saw the bare rock of the citadel, still blackened with the fires of Persia. Nearly twenty-four centuries had passed since the masterpiece of the first of dramatists was produced in the theatre scooped out in the side of that cliff. It was probably some fifteen or sixteen centuries since the Trilogy had been performed at all, and yet, in spite of the birth and death of languages and peoples, in spite of Christianity, and gunpowder, and steam, so slight has been the change in the European mind that the old play never failed of its appeal. To a Stratford audience the setting had not the same significance as to the citizens who crowded to the seats under the shadow of the goddess who gave the casting vote for mercy. Just round the western corner of the rock those citizens knew they could visit the very cavern into which the Furies disappeared, and could offer to them there black victims and watered honey. By the sacred road over Parnes they themselves could start next day for Apollo's temple and hear such comfortable words as Orestes heard. And far away over Salamis they could see, not the blue Malvern hills, but the mountain peak where once the beacon blazed, heralding to the queen in Argos her lord's return in triumph from the long siege, and bidding her prepare the purple carpets for his feet, and the bath for his wearied limbs, and the entangling net, and the two-handed axe that strikes down the king of the herd in sacrifice.

But the underlying motives of the drama retain their power. The curse still passes from one generation to the next. Men and women still love

outside the arrangements of the law. A sudden
vengeance still strikes the proud in the moment
of triumphant security. Men still expect to find
a loving welcome in their homes, though they have
done nothing to make it likely. The murder of a
king and husband is still a terrible thing, and it is
terrible to drive a sword into the breast that nursed
you. Penalty still follows crime, and worse than
penalty is the stealthy foot of Remorse, always
padding close behind the soul and making a terror
even of sleep that is beloved by all. But more
powerful even than the dogs of conscience are the
cleansing powers of Time—

" Time cleanses all—Time that grows old with things."

And still there are higher laws that override the
law, and still there are spirits of atonement and
reconciliation that restore the sunlight to the unhappy. For " Wisdom is child of pain, and born
with many a tear," but Wisdom comes at last, and
Night's childless children are put to rest in the
sanctuary of their dark, primæval cave.

Mr. Benson necessarily cut out much in each of
the three plays that form the acts of the Trilogy.
At full length they would have taken nine or ten
hours in the original Greek, and Mr. Morshead's
translation, excellent as it is, multiplies the number
of words, as is the English way. But on the
first night the performance lasted only three and

a half hours. The only part that dragged a little was the interval between the first appearance of Orestes to his mother and the final scene where he takes her by the throat and forces her slowly back into the blood-stained house. The Nurse is there introduced with a summons to Ægisthus, and perhaps Æschylus intended her as a moment of relief in the horror; for she is almost the only touch of comedy in his surviving dramas. But in this version the comedy was cut out, and the Nurse was made so young that when she tells the Chorus she tended Orestes as a baby, one only expects them to say "Never !"

The treatment of the Chorus is always difficult and interesting. Mr. Benson keeps it on the level orchestra, above which there is a raised platform in front of the palace and the temple ; and even in the cavern at Delphi there is a stage where Apollo suddenly appears in brilliant light. But the main actors come down from the platform and mingle with the Chorus, as was certainly the manner in the poet's day ; in fact, the existence of any raised platform or stage at all at that time is doubtful. But Mr. Benson has new devices for breaking up the monotony of the Chorus. He gives the leading words, in the odes as well as in the dialogues, to various speakers, abolishing the old office of the " choregus," and only at certain passages is the whole Chorus heard chanting together. Another excellent improvement on past revivals is that he does not allow the odes to be sung entirely to music. Large parts are recited just to the murmur of a harp or the breathing of a flute, and these parts were audible and had a strong effect.   As usually happens, the words in the musical passages were barely distinguished, and it is no slight on Mr. Christopher Wilson's music to say that, on the whole, the drama is better without any music, which drowns the words and ruins the work of the poet, as practically all modern music does.   Æschylus himself had taken special pains with the Chorus ; indeed, in his time it was still the most important part of the drama.   He had secured variety by ˊchoosing old men as Chorus in the *Agamemnon*, captive women from Troy in the *Chœphori*, and the Furies themselves in the *Eumenides*.   In the last case his Chorus seems, at first, hardly to represent the average decent person, as most Choruses do ; but, in reality, the Furies do uphold the moral code of ordinary respectable society, and proclaim the duty of vengeance and legal penalty which the average man regards as the base and stronghold of virtue, until some new revelation of genius slowly suggests a higher vision of things that do not work by rule.   Yet it was in the mouths of the Chorus that Æschylus set his noblest poetry, like the great lyric where the dream of the beloved

> " vanishes away
> On silent wings that roam adown the ways of sleep."

or that other in the " Libation-Bearers," which
begins (so like the love chorus in the *Antigone*)—

> " Many and marvellous the things of fear
>   Earth's breast doth bear,
> And the sea's lap with many a monster teems."

And when a poet does say things worth hearing, it
seems a pity that even the best music should make
them inaudible.

Scenery and staging are trivial matters, and Mr.
Benson made no attempt at archaic accuracy ; but
something might have been gained with very little
more trouble.   The debased statue, perhaps a Pom-
peian Bacchus, that did duty for the Apollo to whom
Cassandra prays, was more suitable for a *café chantant*,
and there was no touch anywhere of the austere art
of early Athens.   The arrangement of the dead
bodies of Agamemnon and Cassandra, when the
purple curtains are thrown open, was awkward, and
the repetition of the scene with the bodies of the
Queen and Ægisthus—the one weak point in all
the drama—was hardly better managed.   Though the
poet set the play in Argos, one inevitably thinks of
the Lion Gate of Mycenæ as the spot where the
conqueror's chariot drove up and the maddened
prophetess smelt blood upon the air and heard the
wailings of ghostly children.   It must have been a
temptation to construct a solemn setting out of those
prehistoric stones, but the palace was simply a classic
building of no particular date or style.

These are insignificant things ; and the daring
venture of treating the drama as a whole was
splendidly successful—a success especially welcome
to Mr. Benson himself and to those who saw his
first great achievement upon the stage when he
played Clytemnestra in Balliol Hall twenty-four
years ago. All night the audience were haunted by
that murdered king who feared prosperity too great
for mortals, by the queen who led him along the
purple with lines beginning "There is a sea, and
who shall stay its springs ?" by her prayer that in
her deed of blood the curse upon the house might
end ; and by her ghost hounding on the Furies
against her tormented son, "dark blossom of a
bloody seed."

But in the morning the sun shone upon the
white blossoms that hung on the boughs, and down
the ancient streets the morris-dancers came, and a
procession of Libation-Bearers was formed, carrying
primroses and daffodils, rosemary and bay, to the
grave of our English poet, the one peer of that
ancient Greek.

The " Alcestis " at Bradfield

IT is the comedy of the conformist conscience. Nothing more than that. Columns
of scorn have been poured upon Admetus,
but really he was no worse than the average
unimaginative man, placed for once in an unusual
situation—a situation where the established guides
for conduct failed. We do not like to see a man
trotting round to all his friends and relations in
turn and asking them to die for him. There is
something Chinese about it. But then, in England,
so few of us have had the chance of getting
such a request granted, and so few of us have
known how unpleasant it is to stand on the very
edge of death when we are in perfectly good
health and still comparatively young. Let no man
boast how he would behave at such a crisis till
he has tried. Far from being a scoundrel or a
reprobate, Admetus was exactly "a good sort"—
easy-going, kindly, eminently hospitable, a good
husband and father, carefully observant of all the
essential decencies of life, the requirements of public
opinion, and the obligations of a responsible position
in the country. By Apollo he is called holy as

himself. His very reward of dodging death he won by good-naturedly allowing a god to keep his sheep. Even in his deepest grief he remembers what is due to guests ; he receives Heracles with royal courtesy, and, being prudent as well as polite, he reflects at the same time that, if ever he pays a visit to Argos again, he will find Heracles useful to him there. Amidst his natural and heartfelt lamentations for the death of a wife to whom he was dutifully attached, he does not allow his grief to make him forget the necessity of ordering the Court mourning. With the accuracy of a perfect official, he arranges every detail, down to the clipping of the horses' manes. To the dying woman he vows he will never marry again ; he will love her statue only ; and, as he returns from her funeral, he keeps his vow, though exposed to some temptation. It is more than kingly. It surpasses the saying of one of our own beloved kings to his dying wife, " I shall never marry again. I shall have mistresses."

As men and kings go, Admetus is no worse than anybody else, but rather better. He is the conformist, and the Chorus keeps his conscience. The Chorus, upholding the standard of public opinion, never dreams of blaming him. They congratulate him heartily upon having so excellent and obliging a wife. Though they are old men themselves, they rather wonder that his father, being an old man, did not take her place as the sacrifice, and they do not like to listen to the old father's bitter expostulations when such a thing is suggested. But when all is over, they cheer Admetus up by telling him again and again that such things are common: he is by no means the first to have suffered such a loss; why, they themselves knew a man once who lost an only son, and got over it quite nicely. Of blame or satire there is never a word. They represent the atmosphere of the unimaginative man, the social rules which the good conformist obeys.

Even the old father himself, who is the shrewdest character of the lot, boldly taunting his son with cowardice, advising him to marry often, so as to get more wives to die for him, and frankly admitting that, old as he was, he would never quit the sunlight for such a man—even he, as his ultimate defence, appeals only to law and order. He had never heard of any statute or recognized custom ordaining that fathers should die for their sons. If he had, we gather, he would have considered the question more seriously. But, as things stood, he was the father of his son; he was not going a step beyond what convention required of him.

In the midst of this gallery of worthy people stands Alcestis. I know all that can be said in her praise—this type of wifely duty, this ensample of womanly self-sacrifice. I remember "Euripides the human" and those horrible "droppings of warm

tears." I have pondered on that charming Balaustion's commentary—how the soul of Admetus was
redeemed at last by a woman's utter devotion, and
the test laid on him by a toiling hero. I should
like to believe it all. It would be very satisfactory.
But when I find in Aristophanes that Euripides was
regarded as a kind of Ibsen in his time, and when
great scholars, like the Warden of Bradfield, tell us
the play is essentially modern—the most modern
in spirit of all Greek dramas—then one begins to
apply modern, though obvious, judgments to it.

And in the first place, one finds that Alcestis no
longer loves her husband—no longer cares about
him. Throughout the play she does not say one
word about love. The excellent translation made
by the Bradfield boys makes her speak of love when
addressing her bed, but there is no hint of it in the
Greek. She remembers the time when she did love
him, but that is quite a different matter. Now she
only loves her children, and, apart from her natural
shrinking from death, her chief thought is of the
cruel stepmother that may succeed her. Of grief at
leaving her husband she shows no sign whatever.
I do not say that she welcomed the opportunity of
parting on decent terms from such a worm, to all
eternity. She did not think him a worm ; she knew
him to be what he was—the born conformist, the
average unimaginative man. And her motives were,
in reality, very much the same as his. She is guided

entirely by public opinion. She gives herself up
because she thinks it is expected of her as a noble
wife. She is perfectly conscious of the value of her
sacrifice, and constantly refers to it lest it should be
overlooked. She is particularly anxious that her
husband should realize its full extent. Like her
husband, she is always wondering what people will
say, and she finally extracts considerable consolation
from the thought of her posthumous praise. Her
action, great as it seems, was the grudging and
unwilling sacrifice of a conformist woman.

But if there is one thing more certain than
another in human affairs, it is that an unwilling
sacrifice is of no avail. To be of any avail, a sacrifice must be so permeated and transfigured with
passionate affection that it becomes the only thing
possible and the one thing pleasurable. Then, when
it reaches the height of joy, transforming the world,
it rises into a great action. If Alcestis could have
said, " I love you so much that dying for you would
be nothing, if only it did not part us ! " But as it
is, she had much better have said, " As you ask me,
I think you should do your dying for yourself, and
I hope it will prove beneficial."

Then comes the jolly miracle, and she is brought
back from the grave. As though to make sure that
no one should miss the intention of the play, the
poet brings the rollicking deliverer drunk upon the
stage. That drunkenness is like a burst of air and

sunshine into the stuffy atmosphere of an afternoon
tea-party. It is the appearance of Falstaff in a
churchwarden's drawing-room. Something, I think,
is gained—not so much as Balaustion said—but still
something. Was the play ever the middle drama of
a trilogy ? I suppose not, but one would like to
hear Euripides take up the story from the third day,
after which Alcestis, returning to her household
duties, was allowed to speak again and say what she
thought of it all. Perhaps the tragedy of the conformist conscience would begin there. For I fear
that of that household, as of most, one might say,
" Neither would they believe though one rose from
the dead."

Such were the thoughts that flitted through our
minds as we watched the admirable performance of
the Bradfield boys in their famous theatre on the
hillside, while the song of free birds mingled with
the commonplaces of the Chorus and the martins
kissed each other shamelessly above our heads.
Acting, music, stage-management—all was good.
Death and the boy-child were excellent. But to me
the triumph was a piece of by-play on the part of
Admetus. Just when Alcestis had been carried
away dead, and he was in the midst of his lamentations, he sat down and tied up the thong of one of
his sandals, for fear the citizens should think him
too carelessly dressed for so painful a domestic
bereavement.

Dramas in Whisper

THE rapidity with which Mæterlinck has won a place among the modern writers of Europe is partly a sign of the welcome, which all who are not case-hardened in formalism gladly extend to the least evidence of originality in treatment or theme. Yet originality alone does not hold a position long. We must remember what Goethe said : "The mark of genius is not originality, but sincerity." The real question about an author or any artist, when once we have got over the attraction of his peculiar method or subject, is whether he has enough sincerity to keep us any longer listening to what he says. Has he really anything to say ? Does he in his heart and without self-consciousness believe that it is of importance for him to say it ? Has he the insight that only comes of sincerity ? Can he perceive a fresh truth unseen by the thousand others who have observed the same things as he ?

Those are the questions we ask before we admit any one to the rank of genius, or even of power. For the creative gift is not entirely a thing of brains. It cannot be caught by cleverness or the most elaborate devices, but springs from the whole man, and is the fruit of his temperament, disposition, and unconscious nature at least as much as of his intellect and mental efforts.

Mæterlinck appears to stand the test. He is not only original, but sincere. At first people were interested or amused by his queer manner and unearthly staging. They applauded or laughed, but, like the "Wedding Guest," they could not choose but hear. He has now passed through the fires of progressive admiration, ridicule, and parody. Perhaps no one but Walt Whitman and Ibsen has ever afforded so irresistible an opportunity for burlesque. But we are well accustomed now to his peculiarities. They can neither attract nor repel us more, and still we find that he keeps his hold. He has something to say, and it is of importance. He sees a fresh wonder upon the old face of humanity, and to all who can tell us of that we listen.

The three little dramas called *Alladine and Palomides, Interior,* and *The Death of Tintagiles* were written some years ago, just after *Pelleas et Melisande,* and before the first series of the essays had appeared. We find in them the same strange atmosphere to which we had grown accustomed in *Pelleas* and *L'Intruse.* We are in a region of no fixed place—a region that this world never saw. It is a region such as Arnold Böcklin, perhaps, might paint, and many a child describe. A castle stands upon a cliff. Endless galleries and corridors and winding stairs run through it. Beneath lie vast grottoes where subterranean water throws up unearthly light from depths where seaweed grows. A castle stands in the pit of the hills ; the air around is poisoned, and the wind murmurs strangely in the crevices. Doors open of themselves, and close so that none can open. Or we are simply outside a house in the country, not far from a river. Inside, the family of parents and children sits in evening tranquillity, and we watch them through the window-panes. All is quite simple and uncomplicated. The scene is stripped of cumbersome reality. We move in a grey and abstract world of ideas, just embodied, and no more. It is the home of man without accessories or distractions—a fit stage for these dramas in black gauze.

Upon that stage move human figures almost as abstract—a king, a stranger, an old man, a sister, a queen invisible. They too are simplified from all the variety, the rapid lights and shades, and innumerable motives of common life. They are painted in no other hues but black and grey and a thin pale gold, which is the emblem of beauty, love, and unhappiness combined, as in these plays, alas, they are combined invariably ! The marvel of the work is that with such means effects almost terrific in their power can be produced. Here is the might of simplicity. Surrounded by the naked types of humanity, we are bidden to look into the truth of common things. That the stage may nominally be filled with kings and queens and impossible castles does not make the themes less common. They are the simplest human emotions—the love that comes too late, or robs another of an illusion, the pathos of fancied security, when calamity is knocking at the door, and the passionate affection which dashes itself vainly against the barrier where death is pushing home the bolts. The very heart of humanity in its suffering is laid bare, and we are compelled to peer into it. At times the tension of watching these tragedies of the commonplace—things that are happening in every street—becomes almost unendurable, and we are driven to cry out, "These deeds must not be thought after these ways : so, it will make us mad."

Alladine and Palomides is like *Pelleas* in theme. A restless old king has sought vainly for satisfaction by marriage with a maid from Arcady. In the castle with them dwells his one remaining daughter, the sweet and true-hearted Astolaine, whose lover, Palomides, comes to wed her in the first scene. The plot is at once obvious. We can see the meeting of the lover and the young queen, the sudden change of love in one and the overpowering first growth of it in the other. All the art lies in the peculiar intensity of the working out. "Women do not understand," sighs the old king, "that years cannot separate heart from heart."

L

And when the lover says to Astolaine, "I love you, too, more than her whom I love—Are you crying, too?" she only answers—

"They are little tears. . . . Let them not sadden you. . . . My tears fall because I am a woman; but women's tears, they say, are not painful. . . . See, my eyes are already dry. . . . I was well aware of it. . . . I knew I should soon be awakened. . . . And now that it is over I can breathe more freely, for I am no longer happy. . . . That is all."

The old king in madness shuts the lovers up, bound and blindfold, in underground caverns. They force their way to each other, and are happy in the unearthly light cast up from a depth of sea beneath them, till the lover's sisters, seeking to rescue them, let in a gleam of sunshine from above, and, rather than face the glare of reality and the outer world, they fall into the water together, and are dragged out, soon to die in chambers side by side, calling to each other that illusions have gone, but love remains.

In the grotto, with its unreal light and deceptive jewels and flowers, one can hardly deny the presence of symbolism, much as we prefer to take art of this kind quite simply for what it appears. We regret the symbolism, and, more still, we regret the want of humour which in Mæterlinck so often allows the enemy to triumph. Remembering a passage in *Pelleas* where the sheep go by, weeping great tears, we would warn him to be careful about sheep in general. For Alladine had a little lamb with human eyes and a most sensitive nature, and wherever Alladine went the lamb was sure to go, till she wanted to cross the drawbridge with her lover, and then the creature very properly jumped over into the rushing moat and disappeared. When the two lovers are taken from the deep and seen to be dying, the doctor suggests that the water may have been poisoned, for—

" The decomposed body of Alladine's lamb has been found there.—I will come again this evening."

No doubt that is all very excellent symbolism, but it is grotesque past endurance.

The single scene called *Interior* is even finer than the longer play. In form it is much like *L'Intruse*, and it possesses all the terrible reality of *Les Aveugles* — terrible in its commonplace and intensity. For it turns on an event which might happen any day, and hardly receive a line of notice from the local papers. A young girl has been found drowned in the river. She had gone on a visit, and it is not quite certain how she fell into the water, but a few trifling signs point to suicide. From the garden we see her family, unconscious of the disaster, seated as usual in a lighted room—the father, the two sisters busy at embroidery, and the mother with a little boy asleep on her arm. Bearers are bringing the body slowly towards the house, accompanied by the suppressed murmurs of a village crowd. A stranger and an old man, wet and muddy from pulling the child from the water, stand in the garden, gazing upon the peaceful family within, and wondering how the news should be told.

That is all; yet the realities of that simple situation, the strange significance which now attaches to every movement of the unconscious figures in the room, the terror of calamity's inevitable approach, are analyzed or suggested with such skill that, like the villagers when they arrive, we can hardly endure to think that it is true, and we long to induce the old man to put off the blow for at least another night. Suddenly the family are seen to start and turn their heads. We know that the old man has knocked, and it will soon be all over now.

There is the same irresistible power in *The Death of Tintagiles*, the story of the poor little heir upon whom the invisible queen lays her clutches, no matter how closely his sisters may watch and keep his dear body so safe between theirs that he is entangled in their hair, and the queen's servants must cut him loose before they can bear him away to his mysterious doom.

It is the terror of the commonplace reduced to abstraction. The ordinary situations of life are raised to a higher power by the very simplicity of their setting, and we are compelled to realize the poignancy of emotions which are generally stifled out of consciousness by the unimportant details of existence.

From Leith to Samoa

THE biographer of Stevenson is at once met with the peculiar difficulty that there is little to say—not, certainly, for lack of material, but because the whole story is known already. To readers of his works there is nothing new to be told. Among English writers we do not know if there is any who has more consistently revealed his personality, though perhaps Charles Lamb and Carlyle may be called his rivals, and Byron is not far behind. We do not mean merely that the man's nature seems to shine through nearly every page he wrote. That is the same with all essayists in some degree, and with nearly all poets and imaginative writers. But like Charles Lamb and Carlyle, and Ruskin too, Stevenson always shows a conspicuous delight in dwelling upon the details of his own past, especially of his early boyhood.

We doubt if any other writer, even among those just mentioned, has ever retained so clear and, as it were, so continuous a memory of his childhood. All the emotions, illusions, and happiness of a child remained within easy call of his mind. In a sense, all his best work is reminiscence of himself. Cellini has told us that a man of active and varied life might begin to write down his memories after forty. Montaigne followed the same example. But we find Stevenson writing deliberate autobiography at twenty-nine, though his life had not been active or particularly varied. Before he was halfway across the bridge of life, he wrote of early comrades and scenes in the tone of an aged man, regretful of far-distant days which to him alone are visible and near. If we include his letters, we doubt if any autobiography has ever been so complete as his. It is true he gives it us all in essence, etherealized by the beauty of his mind and the wonder of his style, transfigured and illumined, raised, as it were, to the power of poetry. But it is all there : even the dates and names and places are there, if we care to look for them. Perhaps it was the shadow always standing at his side which kept the quick scenes of each day so vividly in his mind, and urged him thus early to chronicle himself, because at any moment the tablet of memory might be wiped blank, and no one behold its fair pictures for ever again. To this may be due that passionate clinging to childhood, to boyhood, to every brilliant hour of a life that was sure to be so short. The price he paid was high, but ours is the advantage, for we have gained some of the sweetest verse, not indeed for children, but of childhood ; we have gained some of the most delicate essays of remembrance, and a few brave stories that breathe the very spirit of youth.

For the biographer it is another matter. He finds himself hampered with material already used, and used with effect which he cannot rival. The weakness of nearly all biographies is their patchwork, their want of connection. Readers demand the external events of the life, the travels here and sojourns there, though as a rule these have very little to do with the personality. But in Stevenson's case there is the further difficulty that the true biography of his spirit must necessarily be a patchwork from his writings. We do not see how Mr. Graham Balfour could have helped it. Except for one small slip, he has composed the " Life " with every possible care. He tells us exactly the date of each remove made by this charming voyager through life, and the places where he went. He gives us a good deal that will be new to many about the friends in whom Stevenson found his greatest satisfaction. And, above all, he draws for us a delightful and intelligible picture of the South Sea home and the life there, which for two and a half years he had the joy of sharing. This is all so much gain, though a good deal of it is unimportant, as the greater part of external biography always is. But when he comes to the real history of the soul, Mr. Balfour has hardly anything to tell which will be new to readers of Stevenson himself. A few quotations from the diary of her son's doings so lovingly kept by his mother, a few passages from his own diaries, note-books, and unpublished drafts—those who have read the "Edinburgh edition" will find little else that is fresh to them. This is no fault of the biographer's. It was inevitable for the reasons given, and we never expected anything else.

But Mr. Balfour has gathered up the story with great skill. Even to Stevenson's oldest admirers, though he can bring forward nothing that will increase their affection for him or change their estimate of his powers, he gives the opportunity of reviewing in concise form a career of extra-ordinary charm. Of all men of letters we may put Stevenson side by side with Tennyson and Browning, as among the happiest and most for-tunate. There is nothing of the "Newgate Calendar" in Stevenson's life, and something saved him from that Tragedy of Errors which is the common fate of genius. What was it saved him? Let us first remember what a fairylike Fortune waited on him throughout. Born within touch of poverty, but above its grasp, sprung from parents of strong and distinctive character, and brought up among scenes of stern beauty and gallant tradition, part on sea and part among the mountains, he was endowed with a boyhood of the finest quality. Of all his outward circumstance we should envy him most his birth by the water of

Leith and his later home at the foot of the Pentland. He was fortunate, too, in the Covenanter atmosphere, with its tenacious courage and its gleams of gaiety flickering across the consciousness of eternal judgment. The Covenanter nature may not be always very charming, nor always quite sane in itself, but it appears to give a good start for the training of genius. Perhaps it supplies that sanity and seriousness of temperament which genius is tempted to fling away in the poor exchange for eccentricity and self-conscious determination to be conspicuous or socially successful. In his final chapter upon Stevenson's nature, Mr. Balfour very justly writes—

"The gift (*i.e.* the charm) comes naturally to women, and they are at their best in its exercise. But a man requires to be of a very sound fibre before he can be entirely himself and keep his heart single, if he carries about with him a talisman to obtain from all men and all women the object of his heart's desire. Both gifts Stevenson possessed, not only the magic but also the strength of character to which it was safely entrusted."

We cannot doubt that this sound fibre, this strength of character, was largely due to the solemn basis of his upbringing as one to whom eternity rather than the passing day was the true reality of existence. "Something of the Shorter-Catechist," said Mr. Henley in his lines on "R. L. S.," and every one will remember Stevenson's own words upon that subject.

But having thus secured for him a depth and vigour of character, Fortune went on to give him every chance of shaking himself free from all that is petty and sour in the Calvinist mood. His father, himself a man of original mind, with a gift of imaginative language, encouraged him to neglect his lessons and devote his attention to imaginative play. His father also humoured his taste for literature, forced him into no profession, and when literature was finally chosen, saved him from the resource of journalism which would have blunted and frittered his poetic insight. Stevenson was thus able to wander at large through the years when the intellect is chiefly formed, finding a circle of keen-witted friends in London, visiting Paris, dwelling much among the devoted artists of Fontainebleau. Through Spencer, through Whitman, and his friends, as he says, he gained his broad and manly aspect of life, and his early practical work among lighthouses, engineers, and workers on the sea must also be counted in. Before he was thirty Fortune gave him the woman with whom he enjoyed what he calls " the most successful marriage in the world."

Fortune then led him to strange sights and modes of life—to emigrant ships and Californian ranches, to the edge of our Channel, to Highland moors, to Canadian snows, the Spanish Main, and the islands of the South Seas. The very names are

tales of adventure and boyish delight. It is true
that Fortune denied him the active life for which all
men long. Sometimes, though not often, he complained that the shadow of death, which sat behind
him wherever he rode, had not given him a fair
chance. Like every one else, and with an intensity
matching his nature, he would have loved the
soldier's life. When he was five years old, his
mother entered in her diary—

"When made to wear a shawl above his sword, he was
in distress for fear it should not look like a soldier, and then
said, 'Do you think it will look like a night-march,
mama?'"

He longed to take part in war. "There is no
other temptation to be compared to war," he wrote,
"not one." Yet he only once saw even a sign of
the real thing—a mere picquet of Samoan islanders.
Fortune had made him a thin and hectic invalid,
scarcely weighing eight stone at any time. But, as
though in compensation, she gave him a life far
fuller of variety than most soldiers, and almost as
active. She compassed him with friends, and yet
allowed him to see half the globe. She granted
him a disease which in his case, as so often, was
sanguine, hopeful, and full of courage. And she
killed him as suddenly as any soldier can hope
to die.

It was almost a fairylike existence, as though
by magic it were exactly made to suit the man, who

remained half a Highlander in Southern seas, and, to be sure, the man played a large part in the making of it.   In the fate of his writings the same benign fairy attended her godson, who was himself so sprite-like, so closely akin to the "little people." It was, as it were, by the grace of God that he had formed himself before he became popular and famous. All that labour of learning to write, which he has described so minutely, was accomplished, and in fact a great part, if not the greater part, of his best work was finished before "Treasure Island" appeared. If he had never written that or any of his other stories, he would have remained unknown outside the small circle of lovers of literature, but he would still have been one of the distinctive essayists and poets of the language.   In fact, his place in literature would have been much the same as it now is. "Treasure Island" and "Kidnapped" brought him fame and wealth ; they induced many to read his other works ; but it was in his essays and poems that his true power lay.   Had he sprung into fame earlier with those glorified books for boys, there is a danger that he might have neglected his better work and gone on wasting his time to please the public upon a series of such indifferent performances as "Catriona."   As it was, he had made himself an essayist and a poet before the temptation came, and those he never ceased to be, though for our part we would give a dozen "Catrionas," "Wreckers,"

and "Ebb-Tides" for another page of "Virginibus
Puerisque" or "Underwoods." But then we remember "Weir of Hermiston," and if the practice
of story-telling was leading up to what that fragment
promised to become, it was worth a big sacrifice,
even of gifts so rare and fine as an essayist's and a
poet's.

In the time of "Treasure Island's" appearance
Stevenson was fortunate again. George Eliot had
been dead only a few years, and her extraordinary
talent still dominated the novel. Readers rather
chafed under the high tension of her work. Critics
were beginning to grumble, but then they could not
write. Suddenly "Treasure Island" appeared, and
people rushed upon it with a sense of escape and
youth renewed. One new fact in Mr. Balfour's
book is of much interest to myself. The delight
of "Treasure Island" has always been marred to
me because the chart would not work out with the
text. We now learn that the first chart on which
the book was written was afterwards mislaid, and
the present chart was built up from the text, and
unfortunately built carelessly and wrong. This was
done in the elder Stevenson's office, and we gather
that Stevenson himself had no hand in it, and is not
responsible for the mistakes.

And of his longer finished stories, "Treasure
Island" and "Kidnapped" are certainly among the
very best, though we could make up a volume of

the short stories to match them, and, we think, to surpass them. " Jekyll and Hyde " stands alone. The best of the tales could be got into four light volumes. The best of the essays would make two volumes. The poems would go into one, though we might space them out for two in compliment to their beauty. Let us say eight volumes in all. It is almost too much luggage for one man's ghost as he steps out for posterity. He will shed some of it by the way, as a soldier on the march sheds his kit. And yet what excellent stuff it all is ! How unwillingly we should see a single book left behind ! It is all so full of cheerfulness and bravery, so full of thought and jewelled phrase, and the keen flame of life ; so free besides from whimsies and megrims and that nauseating pathos in which our popular sentimentalists wallow naked. Eight such volumes in a life that always walked on the edge of death, and fell at forty-four ! It is a splendid achievement.

But we are dealing now with the biography, and our last thoughts may rest upon the quickening personality of the man himself, if indeed we care to distinguish him from his books. In Mr. Balfour's admirable collection of extracts and details we may find several little quotations and incidents which will be new to most people, and help to illustrate some vital quality. For instance, of his generosity, which was more than regal, and, considering his income, was almost equal to the widow's with her mite, here is a simple example—

"In 1877 he had still £800, but owing to misfortunes befalling his friends, in none of which was he in any obligation to intervene, within less than two years nothing of it remained. His income from writing was as yet extremely small. . . . Until 1878 he probably had never made £50 in any one year."

Or, for generosity of a higher kind, take this aphorism—

"The mean man doubted : Greatheart was deceived. ' Very well,' said Greatheart."

As an instance of his rushing spirits, a visitor at Davos writes—

" Once only do I remember seeing him play a game of billiards, and a truly remarkable performance it was. He played with all the fire and dramatic intensity that he was apt to put into things. The balls flew wildly about, on or off the table as the case might be, but seldom indeed ever threatened a pocket or got within a hand's-breadth of a cannon. 'What a fine thing a game of billiards is,' he remarked to the astonished onlookers,—'once a year or so !' "

How deep was his sympathetic insight into truths underlying the commonest things, we may learn from a note written in a South Sea island on hearing a ship's mass-bell clanging—

"How very different stories are told by that drum of tempered iron ! To the natives a new, strange, outlandish thing : to us of Europe, redolent of home ; in the ear of the priests, calling up memories of French and Flemish cities, and, perhaps, some carved cathedral and the pomp of celebrations ; in mines, talking of the grey metropolis of the North, of a village on a stream, of vanished faces and silent tongues."

Of his tenderness and hatred of cruelty, blended as the best tenderness must be with a certain sternness of disposition, we may take two fine examples—

"At Pitlochry, in 1881, he saw a dog being ill-treated. He at once interposed, and when the owner resented his interference and told him, 'It's not your dog,' he cried out, 'It's God's dog, and I'm here to protect it.'"

After one of Dumas's plays, in which a man employs an unworthy stratagem against the woman who had been his mistress, Stevenson himself writes—

"I came forth from that performance in a breathing heat of indignation. On the way down the Français stairs I trod on an old gentleman's toes, whereupon, with that suavity which so well becomes me, I turned about to apologize, and, on the instant, repenting me of that intention, stopped the apology midway, and added something in French to this effect : 'No, you are one of the *lâches* who have been applauding that piece. I retract my apology.' Said the old Frenchman, laying his hand on my arm, and with a smile that was truly heavenly in temperance, irony, good nature, and knowledge of the world, 'Ah, monsieur, vous êtes bien jeune.'"

The Frenchman's was a wise word. To the

end, Stevenson was always *bien jeune*. To the last he retained the open-hearted generosity and chivalry of mind which we like to associate with youth. He retained the golden illusions which are the finest truth ; he beheld the golden light which shines through common things ; he kept the savage rage at wrong, and he kept the charity which thinks no evil. At Vailima, when the islanders of their own free will made a road for him by his house, they called it " The Road of the Loving Heart." It was a road that Stevenson had trodden all his life.

Meredith

ON the 11th of last month (February,
1904), Mr. George Meredith kept his
seventy-sixth birthday, and every one
in England to whom literature is dear
gave him at least a silent thought of gratitude and
affection.

We might almost say of him that he is the last
great Englishman, or the last but one. He is almost
the last of his peers—that shining group of writers
who illuminated the middle and end of last century,
and from this distance, short as it is, already appear
to us like creatures of an ampler time. In him we
may behold, alive among us still, the natural co-equal,
or but the younger brother, of the great gods who
walked the earth as Dickens and Thackeray, Ruskin
and Carlyle, Tennyson and Browning, Gladstone
and Matthew Arnold. And now, except Mr.
Hardy and perhaps Mr. Swinburne, who are both,
happily, younger, there is no one left who can show
a volume of creative work of anything like the same
value and the same range. We are always likely to
think of the age behind us as nobler than ours,
for we judge it only by the grand memorials that

survive when oblivion has mercifully engulfed the rest. But when we see Meredith there and recall the deeds of himself and his comrades-in-arms, we can hardly help feeling like St. Patrick and the whimpering monks when Oisin returned from fairyland and told of the great things he had wrought of old with Finn and his brazen cars among those self-same hills.

Like many others—for, indeed, his kindliness to younger men is inexhaustible—I have seen him once and again in that little house at the foot of Box Hill which will always be associated with his name. The last time I saw him was before his severe illness of the summer, but already he was unable to move from his chair without the help of his gardener—that friend who will be remembered among the intimate ministers of genius. Yet, though the limbs were slowly losing their earlier glorious activity, no shadow of age had fallen upon the soul, and the grand head retained not only its dignity but its fire.

It is essentially a Greek head. It might have been modelled upon those statues of mature and powerful manhood which, in the museums of the world, are now vaguely labelled "a poet" or "an orator." If it is a poet's head, it is a Greek poet's. There is no trace of the weakness, the conscious melancholy, or petulant emotionalism which, unhappily, have been too often associated with the modern idea of poetic appearance. It is the head of a man who, like Sophocles, could have commanded a fleet as easily as write a tragedy, and as well. When we see it, we cease to wonder that the Athenians should have expected their great poet to do both as a matter of course. It is the symbol of a tempered intellect, in which is no flaw of softness or languor—the intellect of a man, and even of a man of action.

There are men of letters who wear a shut-up, indoor look. Their faces are like the windows of a sick-chamber; we dimly divine the invalid and delicately curtained soul within. But the very look of Meredith tells of the open sky, where the sun marches, and the winds pipe, and the thunderclouds mass their battalions. He might have sailed with Drake; he would have made a fine leader of forlorn hopes and a fine hunter. He "blows the horn of the wild old forest."

His is the head of an orator, too—a Greek orator, like Pericles, whose words the historian might have enregistered as an everlasting possession. The great mouth opens almost four square. It is an Attic mask, a magician's cave. A spirit seems to be speaking, not with it, but through it, and on a broad scale of sound comes the voice, full, unhesitating, and distinct to the last letter, like the voice of one who has spoken much among the waves. We feel that, as Mendelssohn said of Goethe, he could shout like a hundred warriors. Perhaps his slowly increasing deafness had made his utterance even more remarkable when last I saw him ; but in earlier days also his words fell rather in superb monologue than in conversation.

There is no effort about the language ; the great sentences are thrown out with lavish opulence—the careless opulence of Nature at her kindest. There is no pausing for figures, wit, or epigrams ; they come of themselves, as water follows water from a spring. It is the style of his books. There is the same concentration, the same fulness, and the same irony ; but it is all simpler because more unstudied ; and whereas some pages of the books have become difficult and dark, the effect of the spoken word when first it is uttered is wholly illumination and delight. He appears almost to think in pictures and symbols : a comely lady and mature becomes to him at once "a calm autumn day—and in the morning." In speaking of society conversation he at once sees a flock of sheep jumping a ditch in turn ; a burst of laughter makes a gap ; there is a pause ; then the rest come hurrying over—"some of them falling short, their hind feet struggling over the edge."

But when last I saw him the theme was higher than social satire. He was glowing with indignation at the memory of an insult put upon France by some leading party politician. French books seem to be always at his side. It is easy to see from his works that, next to ancient Greece, France is his heroine among the nations. And now France was ordered to "mend her manners;" France that has taught manners to the whole of the world—any manners that the world has learnt; France that is capable of the very highest things—of the very lowest, too, but still of the highest. The misfortune of England, he declared, has been that the highest class in the country has never been a finely intellectual class, has never really cared for intellect at all. And by their example the whole country has been materialized, and now we are led to our national ideals by aggressive tradesmen. So the denunciation went on, very thunderous for a time, but dying away with parting flashes of scorn.

His highest interest appears to lie far more in the great movements of the world than in what is called pure literature by people who display a superior contempt for politics. He follows the whole course of national or political interests with as much diligence as if he had to write leaders on them every night. I well remember his extreme disappointment when I could not tell him the exact origin of some disagreement between two little South American States, whose very existence was a matter of indifference to almost every one else in England.

One sees the same thing in nearly all his books. The tragedy and comedy of souls is played upon a background tinged with the immense issues of human history. It may be the deliverance of Italy we see, or a people starving under Protection, or a Russian war, or the upward struggles of the English poor, or the Courts of Germany, or the alliance of the Iron Chancellor with Lassalle. The greatness of the setting is not merely a literary device of contrasts or harmony. It is not even a deliberate attempt to reach beyond the side street and the suburb of civilized existence. But it is a natural quality of the author's being to see things in the large, and to show us the career of Beauchamp or Diana interwoven in the vast loom of earthly life. It is only another side of that breadth of interest and alertness of mind by which Mr. Meredith would have become the statesman of a century, or the hero of an army, if he had been born to statesmanship and war rather than to letters.

He has said of himself with absolute truth that, though his body is old, he looks out upon life with young eyes. And that is one of his most inspiring faculties. He has never lost the sense of hopefulness or the feeling of life's grandeur and worth. He knows what can be made of life by people who will live it to the full. In his books as in his work there is nothing of melancholy or despair, nothing even of the pathos that we saw in great humorists like Carlyle. It is what he calls " the comic spirit " rather than humour that plays through him. And one sign of his eternal youthfulness is his unceasing interest in youth. He will follow step by step the career of young writers or journalists, hardly above obscurity, just as though they were his natural comrades in the field.

Sometimes I have almost wondered whether this bright refusal of lethargy, this eternal youthfulness, that in old age can still say, "We change a sky for a ceiling if we let Romance go," were not a rarer and more enviable quality even than the supreme creative genius which gave us the last meeting of Richard and Lucy, or the parting of Dacier and Diana, or the visit of Victor with Nataly to his wife. That, at all events, was my first thought when I heard a fortnight ago that our king of literature was now seventy-six.

Thomas Hardy

TO compare the man who has created such poignant scenes of pity and terror as the meeting of Troy and Bathsheba over Fanny's coffin, or the discovery of Tess at Stonehenge, or Knight clinging to the sea-pinks upon the cliff without a name, or Jude and Sue turning back unmarried from the altar— to compare such a writer with so undramatic a poet as Wordsworth may seem strange, but the comparison is inevitable. The resemblance has little to do with the obvious love of both for the face of external Nature, and their intimate knowledge of all her aspects in beneficence or desolation. It is not here their secret lies. In spite of their country life and country themes, neither of them has any connection with idyllic art. To them Nature is not the home of prettiness and rustic peace, and their men and women have nothing whatever in common with nymphs and swains. Both love the mankind that lies close to the breast of earth, and is as truly sprung from her as the grass and trees. In speaking of mankind they never lose sight of this ancient world, so full of strange history, so full of unconscious influences and associations, which for generations have nurtured the children of men and form the setting of their lives.   But Nature without man to them is valueless and unmeaning, and even among men of low estate it is for the aristocracy of passion that they are ever seeking—" the aristocracy of passion," to use Pater's fine phrase for the true patent of nobility.

In all Thomas Hardy's work there is something of the grave simplicity of places, like his Wessex, where man has lived long in close relationship to earth and the seasons.   Most of his characters have grown to be what they are by slow and gradual changes, like the woods or the surface of the downs. They are deep-rooted in far-off traditions of the generations which have passed and left them there. At first sight they may appear rather emotionless, or at least stoical, as well as solid.   Their interests and difficulties lie in the normal lot of mankind, as it was in the beginning and is now.   They have the half-unconscious humour and deliberate speech of men who have time to observe the hours, and to whom the world has not been narrowed by journeys and removals through hurriedly shifted scenes. Amid all their drama of events, we hear singularly little exclamation of joy or sorrow, and hardly any wailing or excessive grief.   Little fuss is made over birth and death and the fortunes that may come between.   The earth turns upon her ancient round, man appears upon her surface to run his course, and the eyes of the trilobite that died millions of years ago, stare from the rock into the eyes of the dying.

"Go quietly," says Old William to the choir in the darkness of Christmas Eve. "Go quietly, so as to strik' up all of a sudden, like spirits." And it is by the very quietude of their surroundings that Hardy secures success when the spirits of his creation strike up all of a sudden. For into this quiet atmosphere of ancient life he loves to introduce a soul touched from its birth by something alien, something that reaches out into a world of different experience, whether for delight or spiritual need. Deep in such souls lies some trace of precious but perilous substance, like the thin vein of gold which is not used for its own sake, and spoils the building-stone for use. In all the four great tragedies we find it so— in "Far from the Madding Crowd," "The Return of the Native," "Tess," and "Jude;" and so it is in "A Pair of Blue Eyes," "The Mayor of Caster-bridge," and "The Hand of Ethelberta," which come but little below those other four.

As Lionel Johnson said in his "Art of Thomas Hardy" (that model of great criticism written by one so young and so soon to die), "The one characteristic scene is the great down by night, with its dead in their ancient graves and its lonely living figure." No writer has so penetrating a sense of place; the earth and sky which surround his men and women claim them as bone of their bone ; but, nevertheless, it is in that lonely living figure that the interest centres.   Lonely, not merely in the face of Nature, it moves, but lonely among its fellow-men, impetuously seeking its true kin and its true star, time after time mistaken and beguiled, and seldom finding what it seeks, or finding it too early or too late.

With a strength of construction that has been rightly called architectural, Hardy shows us the development of a soul like this.   Character is fate, and link by link from its small beginning we see the fateful chain of character wrought out.   The end is often sorrow, and the finer the workmanship, the deeper the gravity, and latterly the gloom.   The tendency to the tragic side is nearly always felt, and it is noticeable how often the shadow of the gallows falls across the fields, like a cruel makeshift for some eternal justice.   But part of Hardy's honour is that he disdains to put us off with any fool's-paradise of easy solutions to life's problems.   No Englishman since Wordsworth has heard the still, sad music of humanity with so fine an ear, and none has regarded the men and women of our country with a compassion so profound and yet so stern as they pass with tears and laughter between the graves and the stars.

The Lilliput World

THERE is something ironic and a little defiant in the very title-page of "The Dynasts." A drama in three parts— that is to say, three volumes—and nineteen acts !

Certainly there is nothing Lilliputian about the scheme of a work like that, and our poor little earthly stage managers must turn away in despair. It is only upon the unbounded stage of the spirit that dramas on that scale can be enacted. Mr. Hardy immediately, and rather proudly, admits it in his preface. The play, he says, is intended simply for mental performance, and he thinks it possible that such performance may ultimately be the fate of all drama other than that of contemporary or frivolous life.

In any case, we have here a drama which absolutely departs from all dramatic rules in the stage limitations. In form it is more like the Second Part of *Faust* than anything else in great literature. It is a vision of the world—" a panoramic show," as the author calls it—including every condition of mankind, from kings and conquerors down to the men and women of the field, and haunted by the inexplicable spirits of universal destiny, by the mocking spirits of ironic laughter, and the sorrowful spirits of human pity. We hear these " Phantom Intelligences" murmuring and wailing over the scenes as they pass before us with the sudden transitions and rapidity of dreams, whilst the Recording Angels chant the unfolded scroll, and man struggles blindly along a troublesome course upon his little star.

But the vision does not reveal to us a series of symbolic and imaginary figures like *Faust*. It is an uplifting of the veil from a few quick months of actual history, and it shows us glimpses of things that were actually happening on earth only a short century ago. It is a panorama of the contest of nations that we call the Napoleonic wars. The great conqueror is here again. We see him pacing the sands of Boulogne and waiting in vain for the fleet that was to give him just the twenty-four hours he wanted to strike at England's heart. We see him before Ulm, receiving Mack's surrender, and again at Austerlitz, pounding the crowded ice with his guns. And there is honest George, his enemy, humbly enjoying himself at Weymouth as a man and a father, and looking forward to the games and horse-collars of an English holiday. And there is Pitt, slowly dying under his high purpose ; and, again, we watch Nelson put to sea and walk the deck among the roar and crash of Trafalgar. Interspersed among these great names, we are given rapid scenes from the Wessex we know so well. The stage-coach lumbers along the Ridgeway ; old men with pikes watch the beacon on Egdon Heath ; and boatmen tell how the crew, for want of rum, drank off the spirits in which great Nelson's body was coming home. We listen as they sing a grand Trafalgar song, beginning—

" In the wild October night-time, when the wind raved
    round the land,
  And the Back-sea met the Front-sea, and our doors were
    blocked with sand,
  And we heard the drub of Deadman's Bay, where bones
    of thousands are,
  We knew not what the day had done for us at Tra-
    falgar,
      (*All*)   Had done,
                       Had done,
           For us at Trafalgar."

Such is the stuff the dream is made of. Scene by scene, sometimes in dialogue, sometimes by actions in dumb-show, we are led through the tremendous happenings of ten short months, and the volume—the first part of the drama—ends with the death of Pitt. Tremendous happenings ? It requires some courage to speak like that after watching Mr. Hardy's vision. Never since Lilliput was imagined have we seen the great fortunes and crises of humanity so reduced in size. We watch the clash of armies, the glories of state, and the splendour of ambition brought down to terms of frogs and mice. It is as though we took our stand upon some star to which the sun is but a firefly, and gazed upon this tiny dust-speck of an earth in which certain microscopic atoms were exploding with almost imperceptible noise.

In that tale of such peculiar beauty and sorrow called " Two on a Tower," Mr. Hardy has used the ironic contrast between the passion in two lovers' hearts, and the rushing movements and unimaginable catastrophes in that universe of stars at which, side by side, they spy through bits of glass. But here the insignificant and pitiful side of the contrast is not in the hearts of two poor lovers, but in the continents and oceans of the world, the hosts of conquerors, the doom of kings, and the crowding populations of European empires. The vision opens, and we see them spread out before us like little toys. Queer little figures run about ; they love and hate, they laugh and cry, and make a fine to-do. You would swear they were real. Here creeps the white Austrian army with "a movement as of molluscs on a leaf." There Napoleon shakes his little fist. There goes Nelson with his ships, the passionate love in his heart and the penny cannon in the bow. There are the tiny villagers scrambling up their little hill to see a real match struck upon the tinder. We hear them speak—

" *First Old Man* (shouldering his pike) : Who goes there ? Friend or foe, in the King's name ? "

" *Woman :* Piece o' trumpery ! ' Who goes ' yourself ! What d'ye talk o', John Whiting ? Can't your eyes earn their living any longer, then, that you don't know your own neighbours ? 'Tis Private Cantle of the Locals and his wife Keziar, down at Bloom's End—who else should it be ? "

So they squeak in ghosts of words—all so tiny and far-off that the squeaks of villagers and emperors hardly differ in their value, and when they have said their little say, the clouds of time pass over them all alike. They are swept away and put into their boxes, with one or two little kicks of the limbs as though the clockwork were just running down. Standing on that freezing pinnacle from which Mr. Hardy, full of the pity of mortality, full of its laughter and amazing ways, regards man's course upon the earth, we behold the world spread like a map in miniature—

"The nether sky opens, and Europe is disclosed as a prone and emaciated figure ; the Alps shaping like a back-bone, and the branching mountain-chains like ribs, the peninsular plateau of Spain forming a head. Broad and lengthy lowlands stretch from the north of France across Russia like a grey-green garment hemmed by the Ural Mountains and the glistening Arctic Ocean.

"The point of view then sinks downwards through space, and draws near to the surface of the perturbed countries, where the peoples, distressed by events which they did not cause, are seen writhing, crawling, heaving, and vibrating in their various cities and nationalities."

N

Sometimes we are shown a vision more woeful, perhaps, even than that sight of the nations squirming together like maggots in a cheese. For instance, on the morning of Austerlitz we read—

"At once, as earlier, a preternatural clearness possesses the atmosphere of the battlefield, in which the scene becomes anatomized and the living masses of humanity transparent. The controlling Immanent Will appears therein, as a brain-like network of currents and ejections, twitching, interpenetrating, entangling, and thrusting hither and thither the human forms."

Of that Immanent Will we can say neither good nor evil. Probably unconscious, probably purposeless, it grinds along its way, and men and empires are but momentary manifestations in its changeful history. So with the laughter of irony and the tears of pity joined, Mr. Hardy enacts before us this puppet show of earthly greatness. He says he was driven to the theme by "the provokingly slight regard paid to English influence and action throughout the struggle by those Continental writers who had dealt imaginatively with Napoleon's career." Alas! Among the mannikins of Lilliput, why should the influence of one tiny family concern us more than another's? All are but blood-vessels and ganglions in the unconscious brain which holds the stars and the universal void.

Beardsley

LET us say at once that we think Mr.
Smithers had no right to publish all the
drawings in his "Second Book of Fifty
Drawings," by Aubrey Beardsley. He
admits in his preface that many of them would
not have appeared if the artist had still been
living. Of one he says it is "a picture which
Mr. Beardsley vehemently prohibited my producing
in the first book of fifty drawings." Yet he "sees
no harm" in producing it here, together with others
which did not come up to the artist's own standard.
Such treatment of an artist's work is unjustifiable.
If a man desires to give half a crown to a beggar or a
church after his death, and writes it on a bit of paper,
the law sees that his wish is respected. But if an
artist "vehemently prohibits" the reproduction of
one of his own works—his works which are the
very essence of his nature, and reason of his
existence—it seems that the moment he dies any one
can set his prohibition at naught, and "see no harm."
When a publisher chooses to do this, he is, no doubt,
acting fully in accordance with his conscience, the
law, and accepted commercial morality. We only

say that it is an insult to art as well as to the dead, and we advise all artists in every form of art to make haste to destroy all relics of immature and unsatisfactory work whilst yet there is time. For let them say what they may, or give what injunctions they please, it will be too late to protect their art and reputation when once the earth lies over them, and their friends begin to gather like ghouls around their remains.

The book, like the other two called "The Early Work of Aubrey Beardsley," by Mr. Marillier, and "Aubrey Beardsley," by Arthur Symons, contains one or more portraits of the artist. Far the best, in our opinion, is the frontispiece to Mr. Marillier's collection. It is one of the studies taken by that genius in photography, Mr. Frederick Evans, who was among Beardsley's earliest friends. In it we see again the clear and striking profile, with its large, strong nose, full chin, and projecting under lip. The short hair, brushed smooth on each side of the parting, quite conceals the low forehead. The eye is quiet and cast down. The ear, set rather far back, has hardly any lobe. The face rests between the two perfectly shaped and artistic hands, which yet are clearly marked by the disease which he knew even then was killing him.

It is a portrait that represents his art, except that it looks so young. Perhaps, by a pleasing fiction, we like to connect youth with innocence;

and his art was not innocent, whatever its other qualities. We may read in the face the instinct of beauty, the fastidiousness of the artist, which does not in the least exclude an attraction to peculiar forms of horror ; we may read disdain, and self-assertion too ; we may read irreverence, and a spirit of mockery, but not of laughter. Indeed, there was no laughter in his art—no real laughter in the most fantastic and mocking of his satires. It is a face of genius, but of a kind that Lombroso and Max Nordau would at once fix upon in proof that genius is a morbid growth, an aberration from the average healthy type of impassive man. Have we then settled the account of genius when we have called it unusual, " decadent," or morbid ? That is a solution as useless to criticism as it is comfortable to the dull.

We have no desire to regard Beardsley's work from what Mr. Marillier—unhappily yielding for a moment to the scientific jargon of the day—calls " the embryological standpoint." But every one must be struck with the peculiar development of his art from stage to stage. At first we see the strong delight in old romance, mingled, it is true, with an impressionist realism, seen in such simple and pathetic drawings as the childhood of Joan of Arc among the fields. Over the whole romantic period, the influence of Burne-Jones is obvious. Some of the drawings, such as the Perseus, the Procession of Joan of Arc, and an angel's head, one might almost take for the master's own.

And that influence long remained. It is seen in the beautiful figure on the right of the Magdalen's Litany, one of the artist's finest satires. But the chief expression of this romanticism is in the great though unequal series of decorations to the " Morte d'Arthur." There, perhaps, in the fine simplicity of the decorative borders and frames, in the dignity of solitary figures, riding through the forests, or seated in quiet rooms, we have the best results of the artist's inborn feeling for beauty. Even there we see the development, or, perhaps, the coexistence, of his twofold styles : on the one hand, the thin-spun elaboration and minute complexity of the Vision of the Holy Grail, and of Arthur with the Questing Beast—a method illustrated by the Siegfried in Mr. Smithers' book. And again, we have the broad treatment, the balance of great masses of dark and light, the method with which Beardsley's name will certainly be most associated ; for at once it began to permeate our art, so that now we cannot walk down a street and read gratifying information about cocoa, mustard, and food for babes, without being reminded of his influence, and of those enchanted regions where knighthood roamed, and ladies all were fair, distressed, and kind.

Unhappily, that restless, eager mind, conscious of genius, conscious how short its time was, and how much was left to explore, to suffer and enjoy, tired of romance before it was done with. The task of the " Morte " was too long for a man who had to cram the work and fame of a lifetime into six years. Long before it was ended, he had passed into regions far removed from the tender moon of chivalry.

In a drawing of 1892, we see, perhaps for the first time, that deformed monstrosity, one knows not whether to call it the abortion of man or monkey, which may symbolize his evil genius. The abomination is opening a book, in which is written Dante's inscription to Love, " Incipit Vita Nova." Whether the creature reads in mockery or in bestial stupidity, one could not say. Who shall decide whether to call it satire or cynicism or brute enjoyment unpurified by passion of soul ? That is a question hard to answer in much of Beardsley's characteristic work, through the most productive of his few short years. He is called a satirist. Mr. Marillier says that " in depicting vice he held it up for scourging ; in exaggerating its fanciful side he but accentuated its squalid and horrible reality." Alas ! we are not sure of that. There are unquestionably scenes of plain and indisputable satire, such as " Lady Gold's Escort "—the shrivelled little woman entering the Lyceum between her nine satellites of fools, debauchees, and fashionable prodigals competing to sell their youth. There is satire in "The Wagnerites"—the foul audience, hideous, bald-headed, bare-backed, fattened and degraded with middle-aged sensuality, sitting there in the fashionable stalls to witness the love tragedy of Tristan and Isolde. In "The Repentance of Mrs. ———," a similar theme to the "Magdalen's Litany," the satire is equally fine. In "L'Education Sentimentale" we may call both the loathsome mother and the leering girl satiric. Even the disgust of the Messalina in the streets at night with her maid, or as she stamps upstairs in her open nightgown after the bath, is within the limits of genuine satire. Sometimes there is a touch of tenderness or pity for humanity which raises the satire almost to pathos, as in the sad tailpiece to "Salome," where a satyr and a clown are laying a frail and feminine little body to its long rest in a powder-puff box, or in a "Platonic Lament," or, in a less degree, in "The Death of Pierrot."

Sometimes satire, which, after all, is only the medicine and not the food of thought, disappears altogether, and we are given designs of sympathetic and unqualified beauty, as in the "Venus" and the "Return to the Venusberg" for the Tannhäuser legend. But, as a rule, in the period roughly marked by "Salome" and "The Yellow Book," there is something in the satire which is not genuine, and which vaguely increases the horror of the designs. What is this disgust added even to satire itself—this spirit of the praying angel kneeling in adoration

before the term of a female Pan, and looking round
to leer at us as he kneels, while the guttering candles
burn like thin flames of sin, and the goddess laughs
with the insanity of abomination ?

Mr. Symons comes near it. His essay as a whole
is the best thing written on Beardsley. It would be
excellent, if he would purge it, as he easily might, of
a few sentences so affected as to be incomprehensible,
and of a few feminine absurdities, like " the adorable
artificiality " of the ballet. Mr. Symons says that
Beardsley is the satirist of an age without convictions. We think that is true, but then it might be
said of all satirists. Satire only exists in an age
without convictions. In Beardsley's case we must
go further. His is rather the satire of a man without
convictions, and that is a very different thing. Contrast him with Aristophanes or Swift, or with Juvenal,
whom he read and sometimes illustrated. No one
could imagine Beardsley crying, that indignation
drove him to the work—" facit indignatio versum."
In many of his most terrible designs we feel that
the satirist's heart is too much on the side of the
thing he satirises. His sympathy is with that " sin
transfigured by beauty," that " spiritual corruption,"
those " phantoms faint and eager with wantonness,"
which Mr. Symons rightly finds in his work.

As introduction to the corrupt and perverted
region where such things dwelt, let us remember
the horror of "The Neophyte," or the haunting

temptation of "The Mysterious Rose Garden." Inside that realm we find Herodias, and Salome at her toilet, or dancing the stomach-dance, and the "Marionettes," and Judas as a little bloated old baby, and the adder-tongued, goat-footed amenities of "La Comédie aux Enfers." We have entered a world where the soul, being infinite in its capacity for sin, wearily pursues the sins that once brought it pleasure, but is sick and languid with disgust because no new corruption of its highest self is left it to enjoy. "Ah, where shall we go then for pastime, if the worst that can be has been done?" it cries ; but in its cry there is a tone of modern littleness, a remembrance of the domino, the frillings, the feathers, and the tights which make it more dreary and miserable than the lamentation of "Dolores." From such a region it is a relief to escape to the tragic horror of the dripping head, thrust aloft by a long black arm, in "The Dancer's Reward," or even to the daintiness and lacework of the "Savoy" and the "Rape of the Lock," too wicked in intention though even they must be held for Pope's enchanted epic of frivolity.

Certainly this "wonderful boy," who called up at will visions of all the beauty and abomination of our time, till at length he could hardly distinguish between the two—certainly he gained the reward he so passionately desired. For two or three years he was notorious. Artists and fashionable people talked about him. Debauchees and lovers of beauty bought his books. Such was his reward. Then he died, passing away in the peace of the kindly Church's last sacraments, and holding the rosary between his fingers. It was a fitting end for a soul, at once so reprobate, so imbued with mockery, and yet so capable of much that is highest in beauty and in thought.

The Gentle Craft

O READER, if thou be a severe, sour-complexioned man, pass by. This is no place for thee, but only for the gentle angler, and anglers be such honest, civil, quiet men. For, thanks to Mr. Le Gallienne and Mr. Edmund New, we have now almost the perfected edition of this fair book. Now has befallen its two hundred and fiftieth birthday, and no better present could be made to its eternal youth than so kindly an issue. Since the "Compleat Angler" first lifted its peaceful head, with the quietness of a water-lily, in the fourth year of Cromwell's turbulent usurpation, it has now been reprinted one hundred and twenty-two times. There has been given to the world a new edition for almost every other year upon the average, and to each generation of man Heaven has granted to read it in five and twenty various forms.

That this should be is very comforting to our faith in the human kind. In spite of all gluttony, avarice, jealousy, and murdering hate, there must be some fibre of gentilesse in the living beings who ask for a reprint of the "Angler" every other year, and are content in fancy to exchange the fume and wealth and clatter of this world for the meadows and silver streams. Here they will find their book in as pleasant a form as ever was devised—with introduction and notes sufficient ; and Mr. New's drawings, whether of fish or scenes, so daintily true and fresh and sunshiny as never yet imagination pictured.

One point only we may add to the learned and poetic editor's information. As is well known, there has been nice disputation among investigators whether the shop that the great Angler kept in Fleet Street and at later times in Chancery Lane was concerned in the sale of hardware or underwear, or, in other words, whether our Izaak Walton, friend of saints and saint of anglers, was an ironmonger or a haberdasher by his trade. After some discussion the editor rightly concludes that "in future he must be written down an ironmonger." But he might further have supported this just contention, had he but known (alas, for the limits of man's mind !) that the Worshipful Company of Ironmongers in the City of London do claim the Angler as a member of their ancient confraternity, and possess his most esteemed portrait as the honoured embellishment of their princely and hospitable hall in Fenchurch Street or thereby. That the Company of Haberdashers have summoned up courage to advance any contrary claim we have not heard.

We do not advance these facts in any spirit of sour censure or despiteful superiority, but only for the sake of the Angler's gentle disciples. The edition of so dear a book has pleased us well, for it is pervaded with the pleasant qualities of the Master himself. To some it has seemed strange that a man should have spent his time so quietly with rod and line and milkmaid's song while Naseby fight perturbed the springs of Avon, and the tramplings of Ironsides frighted the perch of Lea. To us it is not so strange. We find in the book a depth of peace which we even attribute to the proximate contrast of war. Of the Angler we may say, with deep apologies to another poet, that he let the legions thunder past, and plunged his float again. It was owing to this very contrast that he was able to produce a book which, as Charles Lamb (his cleverer brother) said of it, " breathes the very spirit of innocence, purity, and simplicity of heart ; it would sweeten a man's temper at any time to read it ; it would Christianize every discordant angry passion."

That the book is of no service as a guide to angling, that no man ever yet caught a fish the easier because of it, is no great matter. Nay, its uselessness is its compliment. What book of useful knowledge is reprinted every other year throughout the generations ? It is only the useless books that mankind loves, and I, who have known the " Compleat Angler " from my youth up, have never tried to catch a fish, though once I secured a barbel by an accident.

A Memorial to Sir Thomas Browne

THE iniquity of oblivion blindly scattereth her poppy. Diuturnity is a dream and folly of expectation. For gravestones tell truth scarce forty years, and old families last not three oaks. Mummy is become merchandise, Mizraim cures wounds, and Pharaoh is sold for balsam. Yet may we not say that the great subsist not in bones, nor are but pyramidally extant? They require not urns for their perpetuation, and their deperdition is frustrated by their accomplishment. In their company we may include the learned and most gentle Thomas Browne, doctor of medicine and knight-at-arms, who by his books and other tractates, bearing record of his nice and elaborate observations, equally useful as entertaining, has exacted to himself a monument more perennial than brass. We think, indeed, that only now have the chiefest of his works attained to the fit plenitude of their renown, and their vitality is still rather progressional than resupine. For this very cause it has at length been determined to collect such donatives and oblations as may suffice for the erection of a collateral memorial in the form of statue, bust, or other effigy, hereafter to be set in the city of Norwich, where amid the drums and tramplings of well-nigh half a tumultuous century he quietly had his habitation. For such object there is no need of iterated clamations to excitate the giving hand ; but in admonition against exiguity of contribution we may notice that the statue's quality will vary proportionately to the sum subscribed, which same may now be paid upon the tables of Messrs. Barclay and Company, of the above-mentioned city.

The art of style lies not in tortuous and complicated nodosity, and curious as the felicity of his phrase often is, Sir Thomas Browne's writing seems most notable for the equilibrium of his sentence, wherein pole answers unto pole, while summer lightning scintillates between. It is that balance of sentence, united with exactness of word, which keeps his work so sweet. Yet we are not of those who think the secret of his vitality may be sought only in his style, nor can we thus separate a man's expression from his soul. In those books of his we find the scarcely veiled autobiography of a most benignant temper, and a mind singularly alert. They were, he says, at leisurable hours composed, and we like well to think of him brooding over their architectural periods in those flat lands made for contemplative peace. Happy he was above all in the society of a lady so akin to himself in body and mind that we are told they seemed to have come together by a kind of natural magnetism. A physician of high repute, he kept his mind open to science and inquisitive of modernity, though always haunted by the shadow of the past. From the birds' nests of the fen to the urns unearthed in Old Walsingham fields, he suffered nothing to escape him. Among the earliest of antiquarians, he was perhaps the first local naturalist, and the Folk-lore Society may claim him as a founder. With admirable patience and fairness of consideration he gathered and examined the conclusions of popular science incorporated in such general beliefs as that an elephant hath no joints, but being unable to lie down, sleepeth against a tree ; that the badger hath legs shorter on one side than on the other; that the basilisk can convey venenation by the eye ; that an antipathy lies between a toad and a spider ; that children would naturally speak Hebrew ; that a chip of the gallows is good against agues ; that a true emerald is colder in the mouth than a false ; and that Noah was the first man that compassed the globe. To these and many other theories of great acceptance and curiosity he applied his scepticism, usually with a negative result ; for he believed in the equability of nature, and was distrustful of such marvels as are not supported by Divine authority. Yet even in science he leapt not at intolerant conclusions, but ever contempered celerity with

o

cunctation. Modest in demeanour, affecting plainness of habit, in conversation always singular, and so averse to sloth that he could not do nothing, he stands before us among the typical inquirers and essayists of our island. Both for contrast and comparison it were pleasant and not unprofitable to juxtapose him to Montaigne, and even if a parallel to Montaigne's far-famed love for his own friend be sought, we may do worse than look for it in the "Religio."

The present moment we consider most happily opportune for the celebration proposed. For in Sir Thomas Browne we find that tolerant sweetness and reasonable magnanimity, for lack of which our Church is now distracted. For an unbeliever tolerance is an easy task, and what credit has an indifferentist for a scorn of sects ? But Sir Thomas dared without usurpation assume the honourable style of Christian, and both by practice and conviction was ever a devoted son of the Anglican Communion. So devout that he could not go to cure the body of a patient but he forgot his profession and called unto God for his soul ; so humble that he could with patience be nothing almost unto eternity, if only he might enjoy his Saviour at the last. He subscribed to the English Church Articles, and (what is a different matter) he observed her constitutions. Yet he tells us that he never called the Pope Antichrist, or Man of Sin. Holy water and crucifix deceived not his judgment, nor yet abused his devotion. He could never hear the Ave-Mary bell without an elevation, nor did he think it a sufficient warrant, because the Roman party erred in one circumstance, that he should err in all. Averse from controversy, he hoped all things, and, like charity, he thought no evil. He doubted whether a good man would refuse even a poisoned Eucharist; and for his part, he would violate his own arm rather than a church. How remote is that sane and sympathetic spirit from the intemperance of those who desecrate altars and dash the crucifix to the ground! It is even as he says: men have lost their reason in nothing so much as their religion, wherein stones and clouts make martyrs. In expiation of such error, let us erect this memorial as a reminder of the reverent charity in which all of us are short. But to keep our eyes open longer were to act our antipodes. The milkmen are up in Suburbia, and they are already past their first sleep in the East End.

If I were FitzGerald!

IT seems a pity that a man of genuine gifts cannot remain content to be himself. We wonder where Mr. Le Gallienne is going to stop. He is like a "quick-change artist." The other day he was ready to suggest improvements to the Creator on the management of the universe. To-morrow we may have his improvements on Shakespeare or gravitation. To-day, in his paraphrase of the "Rubáiyát," we are allowed to marvel at the daring which gives us improvements on FitzGerald. Mr. Le Gallienne informs us that the idea was " not his own unassisted impertinence." He appears to have been assisted in his impertinence by "the originality of the publisher." It was a dangerous complicity, for murder is no less murder because the murderers are two.

Mr. Le Gallienne, indeed, fair play to him, does not wish to shirk his responsibility ; but surely he might have taken the warnings which stared him in the face. He is acquainted with Mr. Justin McCarthy's excellent literal translation in prose. Did he not read this passage in McCarthy's introduction ?—

"It has been done in English verse once and for ever, and to attempt verse again is at best to put one's self in comparison with FitzGerald, which, in the pithy phrase of the great Hellenic humorist, ' is absurd.' "

It is absurd, because FitzGerald reached perfection. One might just as well rewrite Shakespeare's sonnets or the Psalms. We are reminded of the man who wanted to rewrite the " Paradise Lost " in rhyme, and received Milton's fine permission to do it if he liked. At the moment we cannot recall any other poem but FitzGerald's which is both a translation (of a kind) from a remote and ancient language, and at the same time a genuine classic amongst the people with whom the poem lives transplanted. Except the Authorized Version of the Bible, has any other translation ever become a classic? Fitz-Gerald's has reached that distinction. There must be hundreds of Englishmen who can say the whole of those verses by heart, without even a slip in their sequence. Their phrases have passed into the English language. Everybody knows them. Like the Bible and Shakespeare, they can be quoted without acknowledgment. They are complete and sufficient in themselves, and by that poem of only 404 lines Fitzgerald has become what is called immortal in England.

To his successors, in dealing with the original, there were one or two courses open. Every one knows that he merely tried to represent in modern form the central spirit of the older poet. He re-arranged, he put two or three verses into one, he added original work of his own, and the most striking passage in his work—the dialogue of the Pots—rests on the very barest hints ; there is no such scene in Omar. But FitzGerald's quatrains only run to 101.   In all the MS. put together there are, we believe, about 1200 attributed to Omar, and some 500 of these are said to be genuine, though the oldest MS. has little more than a quarter of that number.   It would obviously be interesting to have a literal translation of the whole or the best parts, just to show us what FitzGerald had to go upon. M. Nicholas gave us that in French prose, and Mr. McCarthy in English.   Then Mr. E. H. Whinfield translated a large number (500 verses in all) into FitzGerald's own metre.   The style is often rough ; it is not a poet's work ; but, to judge from the prose translations, each line almost verbally represents the line of the original Persian which is printed on the opposite page.

All these three books are helpful and unambitious. Mr. Le Gallienne might have taken one step further and still caused no offence to any scholar. He might have said, " As a poet, I cannot be tied by these literal bonds. I must follow FitzGerald's poetic method, but for fear of impertinence, assisted or unassisted, I will not touch the ground he has covered.   There is plenty left, and no one need fear to see the classic version tampered with." If he had said that, we should have no quarrel with him. But out of his 214 quatrains, there are about forty which irresistibly recall the master, and, remembering the old familiar lines with their peculiar grandeur, these new turns of phrase work us up into a fever of irritation which inevitably spreads over the whole of the rest, for we are kept always on the look-out for similar offences.

It is difficult to find exact and unmistakable parallels for comparison, because both writers have taken such liberty with the verses, and often we find three or four of Mr. Le Gallienne's quatrains recalling thoughts or phrases which FitzGerald has put into one. But perhaps we may fairly regard the following pairs as renderings of the same original idea. Mr. Le Gallienne writes—

> "Youth, like a magic bird, has flown away,
>   He sang a little morning hour in May,
>   Sang to the Rose, his love, that too is gone—
>   Whither is more than you or I can say."

That is all right, but remember Fitzgerald's magnificent lines—

> "Yet Ah, that Spring should vanish with the Rose !
>   That Youth's sweet-scented manuscript should close !
>   The Nightingale that in the branches sang,
>   Ah whence, and whither flown again, who knows !"

Or take these from Mr. Le Gallienne—

"Yea, love, this very ground you lightly tread,
  Who knows ! is pillow to some maiden's head ;
    Ah ! tread upon it lightly lest you wake
  The sacred slumber of the happy dead.

"What long-dead face makes here the grass so green ?
  On what earth-buried bosom do we lean ?
    Ah ! love, when we in turn are grass and flowers,
  By what kind eyes to come shall we be seen ? "

And compare them with FitzGerald's single verse—

"And this reviving Herb whose tender Green
  Fledges the River-Lip on which we lean—
    Ah, lean upon it lightly ! for who knows
  From what once lovely Lip it springs unseen ! "

Here is a Le Gallienne verse—

"Nor yet shall fail the efficacious Vine :
  Wash me as white as silver in old wine,
    And for my coffin fragrant timbers take
  Of tendrilled wood—(then plant a rose, and dine !) "

And here a FitzGerald—

"Ah, with the Grape my fading Life provide,
  And wash the Body whence the Life has died,
    And lay me, shrouded in the living Leaf,
  By some not unfrequented Garden-side."

We have also followed some of the quatrains through
all the versions known to us. It may be of interest
to quote the four following renderings (omitting
the French) of perhaps the best known of all the

Omar verses. First, here is McCarthy's literal prose—

" Give me a flagon of red wine, a book of verses, a loaf of bread, and a little idleness. If with such store I might sit by thy dear side in some lonely place, I should deem myself happier than a king in his kingdom."

Then comes Whinfield's bald but close imitation—

" Give me a skin of wine, a crust of bread,
A pittance bare, a book of verse to read ;
    With thee, O love, to share my lowly roof,
I would not take the Sultan's realm instead."

Then Mr. Le Gallienne—

" O come, my love, the spring is in the land !
Take wine, and bread, and book of verse in hand,
    And sit with me and sing in the green shade.
Green little home amid the desert sand."

Lastly, with what a sense of relief we come to those classic and familiar lines !—

" A Book of Verses underneath the Bough,
A Jug of Wine, and Loaf of Bread—and Thou
    Beside me singing in the Wilderness—
Oh, Wilderness were Paradise enow ! "

Here we may notice that FitzGerald has brought in the idea of Paradise from another similar quatrain ; whereas he transfers the Sultan to another of his own (" And Peace to Mahmúd on his golden Throne ").

Well, if Mr. Le Gallienne had avoided this patch

of holy ground, which is permanently consecrated to
a far truer poet, we should have no quarrel with him,
as we said above.   Many of his verses are good as
far as they go ; we read them with real pleasure as
long as they do not call the others to mind.   Let us
take the following as fair examples, though the first
line is intolerable in sound—

> " Eternal torment some sour wits foretell
> For those who follow wine and love too well,—
>   Fear not, for God were left alone in Heaven
> If all the lovely lovers burnt in Hell.
>
> " At the pale gate of birth an angel stands
> Singing a lying song of lovely lands,
>   Sweet as a bird each worn and weary lie,—
> The soul believes and takes the angel's hands.
>
> " White as the moon and as the cypress slim,
> O how my jealous heart doth envy him
>   Who calls thee his to love by sun and star,
> Rules o'er thine heart, and owns each little limb ! "

But in our opinion the best verses of the lot are two
which appear to be built on two very slight hints in
McCarthy's prose.   They are hardly to be called
Omar at all, but they suit some modern moods well
enough—

> " Mine is a passion that can never change,
> It is so sorrowful and sweet and strange
>   That even from the very nightingale
> I must conceal it—'tis so very strange.

> " For lo ! I love a woman this strange way :
>   To be as dead without her, yet to stay,
>   A stubborn exile from felicity,
>   Far from her side until the Judgment Day."

Whilst we are in the way with this fascinating subject, we may recall two verses from Whinfield which seem to have escaped the notice of other poetic translators, though we think the second is in McCarthy. The fourth line in both verses is almost worthy of FitzGerald himself—

> " To lover true what matters dark or fair ?
>   Or if the loved one silk or sackcloth wear,
>   Or lie on down or dust, or rise to heaven ?
>   Yea though she sink to hell, he'll seek her there.

> " A shaikh beheld a harlot, and quoth he,
>   ' You seem a slave to drink and lechery ? '
>   And she made answer, ' What I seem I am ;
>   But, Master, are you all you seem to be ? ' "

These are good enough lines, yet Mr. Le Gallienne might, without impertinence, have shown his cleverness in improving them. But he would have been better advised to have left the subject alone altogether. He gives us nothing really new except a slight sense of grossness. England has an Omar of her own. It is short and perfect ; and in poetry we can afford to have (as the advertisement say) one quality only —the best.

An Omarian Service

IN Mr. Heron-Allen's "Rubáiyát," the author appears to us to have done just what was wanted. In his Introduction he gives us an account of the known MSS. of Omar, and quotes at full length all the passages in Edward FitzGerald's correspondence referring to his version. Professor Cowell, who almost alone speaks with personal authority on the subject, also supplies some interesting notes on FitzGerald's method, and then follow the three main sections of the book: first, a literal prose translation, line by line, of the 158 quatrains contained in the famous Bodleian MS. at Oxford, the oldest, most select, and most authentic of all the MSS. known; next, a photographed facsimile of the whole MS. itself, leaf by leaf; and, lastly, a transcript of the text into modern Persian letters, side by side with the original, together with the literal English translation underneath, and on the opposite pages a series of most useful and scholarly notes, with references to similarities or points of difference in the other MSS. and in FitzGerald's own version. After this section, which forms the bulk of the work, comes a complete bibliography of the MSS., lithographs, printed texts, foreign translations, English translations, and magazine articles on the subject.

The book is beautifully bound, and sufficiently decorated. In the English printing—except that FitzGerald's name is spelt " Fitzgerald " throughout—we have only noticed one mistake : on page 148, the famous line, " The Moving Finger writes ; and having writ," appears as " The Morning Finger," etc. Of the Persian text we cannot speak with authority ; but we have compared the translation with the French prose version of 464 quatrains by the Persian scholar Nicholas, and though differences occur, they are nearly all unimportant.

The Persian scholar will, of course, find points of interest which escape the ignorant, and he would be able to criticize where we can only admire ; yet to all lovers of Omar and FitzGerald the English part of the work alone will give extraordinary delight, and it is a pleasure even to look at the little leaves of the original (only four inches high by one and a half broad, if the reproduction represents the full size), and to trace on them the strange markings, flourishes, and dots which look so random, and in reality mean such beautiful things. It is difficult to imagine that those outlandish scratches contain not only the idea, but sometimes the very words of such familiar lines as, for example—

" And Lo ! the phantom Caravan has reach'd
    The Nothing it set out from—Oh, make haste ! "
Or—

" And then and then came Spring, and Rose-in-hand
    My threadbare Penitence apieces tore."

The original, we are told, is one of the most
beautiful Persian MSS. of its age in existence, and
the Persians were particular about manuscript, for it
was the highest eulogy one learned man could pay
to another to say, " He knew the Qur'an by heart,
and his handwriting was very beautiful."   The lines
are written upon thick yellow paper in purple-black
ink, profusely powdered with gold, though the book
does not appear to be perfumed with costly essences
as many Persian MSS. are ; whence we have Fitz-
Gerald's beautiful phrase, " Youth's sweet-scented
manuscript."   The date of it is 1460 A.D., as we
learn from the fine Oriental note added after the last
quatrain—

" Written by the humble slave Mahmud Zerbudaki,
who is in need of the mercies of eternal God.   Finished
with victory in the district of Shiraz, in the year of the
Hijrah, the last decade of Safar, eight hundred and sixty-
five.

" May God protect him from evils."

This date of 1460 A.D. places the MS. about 340
years after Omar's death.   The next MSS. do not
come till about a century later.   There are three of
them in Paris, and as Omar's fame grew with the

years, the number of MSS. increased, and hundreds
of later verses were written under his name.   We
believe there are now in all about 1200 quatrains
attributed to him beyond the modest 158 of the
Bodleian MS.   But of all these later MSS. the most
interesting to us is the "Calcutta," which was the
chief other text consulted by FitzGerald himself.
It contains 516 quatrains, and a good many ideas in
our familiar version can be traced to it.   A certain
number also are derived from other Persian poets,
kindred with Omar.

But it is to this very "Bodleian" itself that we
must look for FitzGerald's main inspiration.   Of his
hundred quatrains, just about fifty can be distinctly
traced to lines or whole verses in this MS.   It is
true that sometimes we only get the hint of an idea.
Sometimes several verses of the original will supply
the material for only one of his.   The idea, for
instance, for the lines—

> " And lose your fingers in the tresses of
> The Cypress-slender Minister of Wine,"

is repeated three or four times by Omar himself.
Less frequently, FitzGerald has built two stanzas
out of one.   Often he has taken a line or two
from one quatrain and put them into another.   And
nearly always throughout he has arranged his stanzas
in some sort of sequence, and given them a connection of which there is, of course, no trace at all

in the original " di-wan " arrangement in a kind of alphabetical order.

But what will probably surprise most of his admirers, even if they are familiar with the excellent versions, in prose by Mr. Justin McCarthy, and in verse by Mr. Whinfield, is the closeness with which FitzGerald has sometimes kept even to the very lines and words of the Persian itself. We have noted, as was said, about fifty instances of fairly exact translation, but a few examples selected from that number will explain the method best. Let us arrange the bare prose translations and FitzGerald's poems in couples alternately throughout, taking the examples as they come in the manuscript—

" Since no one will guarantee thee a to-morrow,
      make thou happy now this love-sick heart of thine ;
    Drink wine in the moonlight, O Moon, for the moon
    shall seek us long and shall not find us."

  " Ah, Moon of my Delight who know'st no wane,
      The Moon of Heav'n is rising once again :
        How oft hereafter rising shall she look
      Through this same Garden after me—in vain ! "

  " They say that the garden of Eden is pleasant to the
          Houris :
      I say that the juice of the grape is pleasant.
      Hold fast this cash and let that credit go,
      for the noise of drums, brother, is pleasant from afar."

" Some for the Glories of The World ; and some
　　Sigh for the Prophet's Paradise to come ;
　　　　Ah, take the Cash and let the Credit go,
　　Nor heed the rumble of a distant drum ! "

" Everywhere that there has been a rose or tulip-bed,
　　there has been spilled the crimson blood of a king ;
　　Every violet shoot that grows from the earth
　　is a mole that was once upon the cheek of a beauty."

　　" I sometimes think that never blows so red
　　　　The Rose as where some buried Cæsar bled ;
　　　　　　That every Hyacinth the Garden wears
　　　　Dropt in her lap from some once lovely Head."

" Although wine has rent my veil,
　　so long as I have a soul I will not be separated from wine :
　　I am in perplexity concerning vintners, for they—
　　what will they buy that is better than what they sell ? "

　　" And much as Wine has played the Infidel
　　　　And robb'd me of my Robe of Honour—well,
　　　　　　I wonder often what the vintners buy
　　　　One half so precious as the stuff they sell."

" O soul ! if thou canst purify thyself from the dust of the
　　　　body,
　　thou, naked spirit, canst soar in the heavens,
　　the Empyrean is thy sphere,—let it be thy shame
　　that thou comest and art a dweller within the confines
　　　　of earth."

P

" Why, if the Soul can fling the Dust aside,
And naked on the Air of Heaven ride,
    Were't not a Shame—were't not a Shame for him
In this Clay carcase crippled to abide ? "

As to FitzGerald's vision of the Talking Pots, several hints for such a scene, and for his other stanzas on the potter and the clay, are scattered up and down the original, but without order or form. We may take one or two instances—

" I went last night into the workshop of a potter,
I saw two thousand pots, some speaking, and some silent,
Suddenly one of the pots cried out aggressively :—
' Where are the pot maker, and the pot buyer, and the
    pot seller ? ' "

This one stanza has been developed by FitzGerald into three, which every one will recognize at once. Or again—

" The elements of a cup which he has made, to contain
    wine,
a drinker will not permit to be scattered abroad ;
all these heads and delicate feet—with his finger-tips,
for love of whom did he make them ?—for hate of whom
    should he break them ? "

" Then said a Second—' Ne'er a peevish Boy
Would break the Bowl from which he drank in joy :
    And He that with his hand the Vessel made
Will surely not in after Wrath destroy.' "

" When I am abased beneath the foot of destiny,
  And am rooted up from the hope of life,
  take heed that thou makest nothing but a goblet of my
      clay,
  haply when it is full of wine I may revive."

" ' Well,' murmur'd one, ' Let whoso make or buy,
  My Clay with long Oblivion is gone dry :
      But fill me with the old familiar Juice,
  Methinks I might recover by-and-by.' "

" The month of Ramazan passes and Shawwal comes,
  the season of increase, and joy, and story-tellers comes ;
  now comes that time when ' Bottles upon the shoulder ! '
  they say—for the porters come and are back to back."

" So while the Vessels one by one were speaking,
  The little Moon look'd in that all were seeking :
      And then they jogg'd each other, ' Brother ! Brother !
  ' Now for the Porter's shoulder-knot a-creaking ! ' "

That, the last quatrain of the Talking Pots, is also
the last of the original MS., and it is evident that it
is one of those which need the notes supplied by
Mr. Heron-Allen on the page opposite the text.
These notes appear to us to be admirably done, for
they are quite short, but sufficient, and perfectly
clear. For instance, the first note on this quatrain
(which even in the English version is difficult without FitzGerald's explanation) is—

" Ramazan is the ninth month of the Muhammadan
year, which is observed as a month of fasting and penance,

during which rigid Muslims neither eat, drink, wash, nor caress their wives. The first day of Shawwal is therefore eagerly looked forward to in the East."

There are a few stanzas which FitzGerald has not used, but which are in themselves worthy of remembrance. As such we may select—

" Khayyam (which means tent-maker), who stitched at the
        tents of wisdom,
    fell into the furnace of sorrow, and was suddenly burnt ;
    the shears of doom cut the tent-rope of his existence,
    and the broker of hope sold him for a mere song.

" If thou desirest Him, be separated from wife and children,
    bravely move thine abode from the relations and friends :
    whatever is, is an hindrance on the road for thee,
    how canst thou journey with these hindrances ? remove
        them."

(Which is a text for Thoreau.)

" Fill the cup ! for the day breaks white like snow,
    learn colour from the wine that is ruby :
    take two fragrant aloe logs, and brighten the assembly,
    make one into a lute, and burn the other."

(Which is a text for Horace.)

" So far as in thee lies, follow the example of the profligate,
    destroy the foundations of prayer and fasting :
    hear thou the Word of Truth from Omar Khayyám,
    'Drink wine, rob on the highway, and be benevolent.'"

(Which is a text for Villon and Robin Hood.)

Omar again

WHEN Oxford's Professor of Modern History speaks, we must listen ; especially if he be a man of the late Professor York Powell's versatility, humour, and energy of thought. Otherwise, one would hardly have cared to notice more " Quatrains from Omar Khayyám." In truth, we have enough of them now, and want no more.

But the Oxford Professor of Modern History came up with his little lot of twenty-four quatrains and an introduction. One thing might be said at once ; he avoided Mr. Le Gallienne's fatal error. There is no verse of his which at once challenges comparison with any particular verse of FitzGerald's. We escape the irritation of that unnecessary rashness, at all events. Out of the 1200 quatrains that have been attributed (for the most part falsely) to Omar, Professor York Powell was most careful not to select any that can be distinctly traced in FitzGerald. On the other hand, his two dozen include many which are perfectly familiar in other versions, and his success or failure may best be judged by one or two instances. Take the well-known quatrain, which

FitzGerald gives only in prose, on Khayyám himself. It is the twenty-second in the Bodleian MS., and the literal translation reads—

"Khayyám, who stitched at the tents of wisdom,
    fell into the furnace of sorrow, and was suddenly burnt ;
    the shears of doom cut the tent-rope of his existence,
    and the broker of hope sold him for a mere song."

Mr. Garner's version runs—

"Khayyám, who stitched the tents of wisdom's lore,
Is fallen in the pit and covered o'er ;
    Death's shears have cut the tent-ropes of his life ;
The world has cast him out as worthless store."

Professor York Powell gives—

"Khayyám, that used to stitch the tents of Thought ;
Into Grief's furnace dropt, was burnt to naught ;
    The shears of Fate his Life's tent-ropes have cut ;
Yea, Hope's sharp Broker sold him—nor got aught."

That is wonderfully close to the original certainly. It only wants the final touch of style—just the imaginative perfection—to make it worthy of Fitz-Gerald. But the master would never have passed that last line with its harsh sounds and wretched ending. Of the three versions, Mr. Heron-Allen's prose, which is practically identical with Professor Cowell's old translation, given by FitzGerald, is surely the finest rendering.

Or, take the sixtieth in the Bodleian MS. ; in Mr. Heron-Allen's prose it runs—

" This caravan of life passes by mysteriously ;
  mayest thou seize the moment that passes happily !
  Cup-bearer, why grieve about the-morrow of thy patrons ?
  Give us a cup of wine, for the night wanes."

For this Mr. Garner has—

" Life's caravan unheeded glides away,
    And barren hopes alone remain—but nay—
      Fear not the pain the future has in store,
    But drink—upon us steals the twilight gray."

Professor York Powell's version is—

" Life's caravan speeds strangely swift—take care ;
    It is thy youth that's fleeting—Friend, beware ;
      Nor vex thyself for Woe to come, in vain,
    For lo, the Night rolls on and Dawn breaks bare."

Except for the needless weakness of " in vain," that
is fine, though not so close as Mr. Garner's.   But
in this case, for once, we may compare the idea, at
all events, with a real FitzGerald.   Take this one of
the only three quatrains, which are really better in
his first version than in their final form—

" One Moment in Annihilation's Waste,
    One Moment of the Well of Life to taste—
      The Stars are setting, and the Caravan
    Draws to the Dawn of Nothing—Oh, make haste ! "

How superb !   What a triumph of language, com-
pact with imagination !

   We will take but one more instance for comparison.   It is a quatrain that does not occur in the
Bodleian MS.   Professor York Powell has it—

> " Above thine head looms Heaven's Bull Parwin ;
> Beneath thy feet a Bull bears Earth unseen ;
> Open the eyes of Knowledge, and behold
> This drove of Asses, these two Bulls between."

For this Mr. Garner gives—

> " A bull there is named Parwin in the skies,
> A second underneath this footstool lies,
> A drove of asses two great bulls between
> This swarm of mortals seems to Wisdom's eyes."

Neither of them is very good, but Mr. Garner's is considerably the more intelligible.

On the whole the verse of Professor York Powell which pleases us most is one of those which he attributed to some other poet than Omar—a man of wittier and more malicious mockery—

> " O Lord, have mercy on my enslaved Soul :
> Have mercy on my Heart that Griefs control :
> Have mercy on my Foot that seeks the Inn :
> Have mercy on my Hand that craves the Bowl."

The second line is weak enough, but the rest appears to us excellent, and in reality quite Omarian in spirit.

As to the Professor's Introduction, it is rather random, slap-dash stuff. We do not gain much illumination from classing Omar with Shakespeare, Goethe, Rabelais, and Whitman ! Nor do we need to be told that Omar "lived far above the haunts

of the mere hog-philosophy." Still less, that "he
was too healthy to permit the eternal verities to
crush him into wanhope and gloom." Wanhope!
O William Morris and Wardour-street, what liberties
are committed in your names!

The Poet of the Sidhe

MAY we say, without fear of violence, that up to now Ireland has produced hardly a single poet who could use English with poetic power? We are far from meaning that the race has been poor in poets. The very name of Irish seems to imply the poetic temper. It is in the blood, whether it find expression in quixotic enterprise, irresistible charm, or in the verse of almost unknown singers and glee-men who sang the Celtic tongue from before the Christian age, down to the ruinous years of last century's beginning. In what Germans and pedants would call " folk-poetry," Ireland possesses a heritage unsurpassed, but to us English it has always been a sealed book, and the penal laws, famine, English education, and even the very open-heartedness of the people, have almost sealed it up from the Irish themselves.

To obtain any hearing at all, Irish poets have been compelled, till quite lately, when they began to write in Irish again—they have been compelled to use a tongue entirely foreign to the race. We know how poor and artificial even Burns becomes the very moment he quits his native dialect, and strives to write English correctly. But the Irish poets were worse off than Burns. They had no comprehensible dialect to fall back upon, and English had been imposed upon them, as a foreign language upon a conquered race, just at the very time when it was least fitted for true poetic expression. It was an age of prose and rhetoric. What superb use could be made of the tongue under those forms was shown by Swift, Sterne, Goldsmith, and Burke. It may still be seen in every newspaper and village meeting through the island. But poets had no chance.

Most Irishmen would agree that, apart from a few rebel songs, the best Irish poetry of last century was written by Moore, Samuel Ferguson, and Mangan. Yet how stilted and untrue the greater part of it sounds to our ears! The medium is evidently a *learnt* language, not a native growth of race. Even Mangan never rose twice to the true poetic glory of the "Dark Rosaleen;" and as to Moore, even the "Irish Melodies" will never rank among the faultless lyrics of our tongue. They are remembered for their tunes. Almost every one knows the first lines, and nothing more: "When he who adores thee has left but the name," "Rich and rare were the gems she wore," "'Tis the last rose of summer," "Come, rest in this bosom"—echoes of our great-aunts' musical evenings—inexpressibly touching for their memories, but not quick with immortality.

With Mr. Yeats a new era begins. He uses our language as the great English poets use it. He has all the tender and assured intimacy of a child sprung from the mother-race—an intimacy which no stranger or foreigner can ever win. He is free-born of the language, and he imbibed its strength at a time when our poets had restored it to its former power. The souls of Wordsworth, Shelley, Tennyson, Browning, and Swinburne have passed into our poetic tongue. Mr. Yeats takes it up from them as their successor, and uses it, like themselves, with the force of natural unconsciousness. In his hands it becomes so different from the language which was forced upon subjugated Ireland, that it can hardly be called the same speech. The rhetoric has gone; the artificial but commonplace diction, so dear to our grandfathers, has gone. Apart altogether from the thought and temperament, any one might think that the language was the work of one of our own great poets. There are, of course, conscious introductions of some old Celtic word or phrase, and in one instance the use of the word "fret" in the Irish sense of "doom" is a little hard on English readers. But that has nothing to do with the change we mean. What we mean is the change from such lines as—

> "Silent, O Moyle, be the roar of thy water,
>   Break not, ye breezes, your chain of repose,"

to the beauty and cadence of the verse—

"Who will go drive with Fergus now,
And pierce the deep wood's woven shade,
And dance upon the level shore ?
Young man, lift up your russet brow,
And lift your tender eyelids, maid,
And brood on hopes and fears no more."

In both these lyrics the theme is an old Irish legend, but, even if we leave the question of language, how vast is the difference in the whole conception ! We rise from a drawing-room ballad under early Victorian chandeliers to a spirit's song among the "dishevelled wandering stars." It is with the same delights in the vanished past of Ireland that the poet has revived so many of his country's myths and traditions. We have seen them in the leaves of "The Secret Rose," and in the volume of revised and collected verse we find "The Death of Cuchulain," recalling the direct and epic manner of Matthew Arnold's "Sohrab and Rustum ;" "The Madness of King Goll," a Browningesque dramatic lyric ; and the great poem of "The Wanderings of Oisin." We hardly know what to compare that to. It has the concrete wealth and rareness (if we may use the word) of Browning's earlier work. There are passages in it which recall the grand lyrics in "Paracelsus"—the galleys that went over the sea, the song of cassia, sandal-buds, and stripes of labdanum. But then, again, we find a loving accuracy more tender even than Browning's. It seems as though not a little mouse in nature escaped the poet's vision. How express and exact, how far removed from the old conventions of rhetorical verse, is the sudden end of the faery lament over the ageing and decay of earthly things !—

> " And the kingfisher turns to a ball of dust,
> And the roof falls in of his tunnelled house."

Over the whole poem there lies a faery glamour, an incalculable strangeness which reminds us of Blake, but has in it that something further of unrest and unappeasable longing which we are obliged to call the Celtic mood, though of late we have been a little overdone with talk about the Celt and his Celtism. That hungry longing haunts the soul of man, so that even in fairyland it is only the fairies who fear not " the gray wandering osprey sorrow." To Oisin even there it came when after a hundred years he found in the foam a staff of wood from some dead warrior's broken lance. Then the ancient sorrow of men took hold on him again—

> " And I wept,
> Remembering how the Fenians stept
> Along the blood-bedabbled plains,
> Equal to good or grievous chance."

No one could deny humour of the best kind to the author of that humorous and pathetic book " The Celtic Twilight ; " but, like the best humour in general, it is accompanied by what he somewhere calls the visionary melancholy of instinctive natures and of all animals. He never condescends to the kind of humour which the English used patronizingly to expect from the Irish as a due and tribute. In the collected poems there is hardly a touch of humour of any kind, even in the few ballads of common life. In the two beautiful dramatic poems of *The Countess Cathleen* and *The Land of Heart's Desire*, there sometimes lies, it is true, a kind of lurking humour ; but we need hardly discuss those dramas here, for the little fairy Mystery is familiar to London playgoers, and *The Countess Cathleen* was worthily praised during its performances in Dublin.

Yet even these dramas are rather lyrical in motive than dramatic in action or character. Mr. Yeats is in essence a lyric poet. He has the visionary insight, the sensitive apprehension of wide human emotions, the unreasoned perception of the dim but entirely real truths of spirit and feeling which lie behind the common surfaces of life. Besides, he possesses the rare and incommunicable gifts of melody and charm. There is no explaining these things. Let us rather remember such lyrics as that beginning " If Michael, leader of God's host " —a poem fit to stand among Blake's " Songs of Innocence "—or " The Isle of Innisfree," or that on the shoes of sorrow, or the unsatisfied yearning of

" The Man who dreamed of Fairyland " and " The Sad Shepherd," or the chill weariness and strange new hope of " Ephemera." Who can tell where lies the enchantment in those four simple verses called " A Dream of a Blessed Spirit " ? They are a piece of holy witchcraft. And, by the way, the new last verse is fine, but we cannot spare the old. Is it impossible to include both ? Otherwise, as a rule, the alterations in the volume are valuable and sometimes necessary, though we regret at least one omission of a whole poem.

We do not know where others may look for the poet's best. Perhaps in the fairy scenes of Oisin, with their songs of delight and sorrow ; perhaps in the fairy child who tempts the bride to life of unfettered joy ; or in the countess who sells her soul for the hungry poor. For us there is a set of poems which stand apart. The most are to the Rose—the black Rose of the olden singers. One begins—

> " Red Rose, proud Rose, sad Rose of all my days !
> Come near me, while I sing the ancient ways : "

And another begins—

> " Rose of all Roses, Rose of all the World ! "

Another tells of—

> " Cabins gone now, old well-sides, old dear places ;
> And men who loved the cause that never dies."

And yet another says—

> " Know that I would accounted be
> True brother of that company,
> Who sang to sweeten Ireland's wrong."

There are many beside. Why, is not the whole book an offering to the Secret Rose, the land which, in all her sadness, ever remains the threshold of that Land of Heart's Desire ? We do not know what better fate could have befallen any poet than to have created so rich a gift and laid it upon the heart of his people.

The Latter Oisin

THE fairies have got hold of Mr. Yeats. It is well known in Ireland how dangerous it is to sleep on a rath, or ancient circle of stones. Some, indeed, have ventured it by daylight without greater harm than visions, but none may safely dare at night, or at the earliest dawn, when the fairies have most power. Unless, indeed, one be ugly or stupid, for then what need should the fairies have of you? It is beautiful children they want, or winning brides, or youths who can dance or sing. Such have no chance, if on a rath they fall asleep, or on a bed of Diarmuid and Grainne, whose beds of hewn rock, called cromlechs by dingy antiquarians, are scattered through the land, one for each evening of their year's flight—and it was Leap-year, too. They come — the fairies, the Sidhe, the good people, shadowy visitants from an elder day; they touch their favourite's heart with their filmy hands, they sing him away. Little by little he pines and fades; he shrinks together; or, maybe, in an instant he is "swept;" he is gone. With the fairies now he dances or he sings. Within a year and a day he

may still be recovered; but if that chance of grace
be lost, he is gone, and never may return.

What fairy of the wild was so full of the passion
of poetry that no one short of Mr. Yeats could
satisfy her yearning for the best? On what rath or
massy granite did he fall asleep? She has him now;
she holds him fast.

> "Habes tota quod mente petebas,
> Inrelix."

With what songs does he delight her, what elfin
echoes of the songs we used to love? She holds
him fast, and we cannot wonder. No poet of our
day sings music like his, so strange, so wild, so full
of sweet enchantment.

Or shall we compare him to Lycidas, drowned
in the Irish Channel, beside the steep where the
famous Druids lie?

> "Where were ye Nymphs when the remorseless deep
> Clos'd o'er the head of your lov'd Lycidas?"

Yes, it was the Nymphs of Greece, so helpful,
and strong, and clear of purpose, that should have
saved him. But of them he has no care.

> "Ay me, I fondly dream!
> Had ye bin there—for what could that have don?"

We must rather liken him to Oisin, of whom he
once so sweetly sang himself, how drawn by the
enticement of Niam, that white witch, he left his
Fenians at their hunting and galloped with her over

the glossy sea to the Land of Youth, whence, after three ages, he returned and found Christ and St. Patrick where the Fenians used to war. And to the saint he strove to tell his woeful story of delight; but the saint made little of it, having his mind set on the stern simplicities of heaven and hell. For the moment we, too, must play the part of saint, and try to find what this "revenant" from fairyland is striving to tell us of.

For he has walked among the seven woods of Coole — "seven odours, seven murmurs, seven woods"—where beings happier than men moved round him in the shadows—

"How shall I name you, immortal, mild, proud shadows?
I only know that all we know comes from you,
And that you come from Eden on flying feet.
Is Eden far away, or do you hide
From human thought, as hares and mice and coneys
That run before the reaping-hook and lie
In the last ridge of the barley? Do our woods
And winds and ponds cover more quiet woods,
More shining winds, more star-glimmering ponds?"

In regions pictured by such lines as must have held all fairyland silent with their melody, a vision comes to the poet of a galley's deck upon a misty sea. He calls it "The Shadowy Waters." Upon the galley's sail are worked three rows of hounds— one dark, one red, one white with red ears, of which we know (though the poet does not stay to tell us) that the last are the ancient symbols of the hounds of death, and the red are for courage. The hero, Forgael, sleeps upon skins, a silver lily on his breast, a magic harp near by, from which a fool upon an island had drawn strange music three months before. And six months before that—

> "Something that was bearded like a goat
> Walked on the waters, and bid Forgael seek
> His heart's desire where the world dwindles out."

So he has wandered north over a desert sea guided by grey birds which are the souls of heroes dead, through regions where red hounds are seen to run from silver arrows. And now the moons of birth are filled, and still he wanders on, so that, but for the magic harp, his crew would destroy him, desiring their return. Even Aibric, his steady follower, urges return now. "No man," he says—

> "No man had doubts
> When we rowed north, singing above the oars,
> And harried Alban towns, and overthrew
> The women-slingers on the Narrow Bridge,
> And passed the Outer Hebrides, and took
> Armlets of gold or shields with golden nails
> From hilly Lochlann ; but our sail has passed
> Even the wandering islands of the gods,
> And hears the roar of the streams where, druids say,
> Time and the world and all things dwindle out."

What is it that Forgael seeks in this region so near akin to nothingness ? He tells us, as in a

vision, darkly ; and in the following lines, if we
will, we may remember that Aengus is the lord of
love and beauty in the Land of Youth, and that
Edaine was lured away from an earthly love into the
Land of Youth by Midher of the Shee, and there
left him to be with Aengus in his tower of glass.
So Forgael says—

> " There is a love that the gods give,
>   When Aengus and his Edaine wake from sleep,
>   And gaze on one another through our eyes,
>   And turn brief longing and deceiving hope
>   And bodily tenderness to the soft fire
>   That shall burn time when times have ebbed away.
>   The fool foretold me I would find this love
>   Among those streams or on their cloudy edge."

Suddenly a strange ship looms through the white
fog, and on board her a strange crew is seen—an old
man, a woman lying on embroideries, a boy and girl
hand-in-hand, a dreaming man with a red crown.
Forgael's men steal upon the newcomer like pirates,
lash their ship to her side, then slay. Above the
mast the souls of the slain flutter like grey birds.

To Forgael the men bring the lady with a rose
on her breast, hoping that in her they have found his
heart's desire. She is Dectora ; we suppose the
same Dectora who was the mother of Cuchulain,
but we are not sure. Now she is seeking help from
the gods to conquer the countries of the north, but
finding only empty waters she has turned home.

She calls on the sailors to save her from Forgael's love, but with his harp and the white birds of fairyland he puts them all to confusion, and they cross to seek the ale and comforts of the other ship. Then Forgael charms the lady into a sleep of forgetfulness, haunted by dreams of a red hound and silver arrows too. Awaking, she kisses the harp, and the twain embrace upon the empty waters.

But, alas for love! A crown glitters beside the oar; a red-eared hound slides past pursuing a hornless deer, and in Forgael the old craving awakes again. She offers him all the love of hands and hair, but he will have none of it. "The love," he says—

> "The love of all under the light of the sun
> Is but brief longing, and deceiving hope,
> And bodily tenderness; but love is made
> Imperishable fire under the boughs
> Of chrysoberyl and beryl and chrysolite,
> And chrysoprase and ruby and sardonyx."

Therefore he refuses love among the winds of the world, and bids the lady seek the comforting love with Aibric in the other ship. Not so she. Cutting their ship loose from the other's side, she vows to follow him even to where the world may dwindle out. Setting the crown at his feet, she puts her arms about him, and then cries—

> "Bend lower, O King,
> O flower of the branch, O bird among the leaves,

O silver fish that my two hands have taken
Out of a running stream, O morning star
Trembling in the blue heavens like a white fawn
Upon the misty border of a wood—
Bend lower, that I may cover you with my hair,
For we will gaze upon this world no longer.

(*The harp begins to murmur of itself.*)

"FORGAEL : The harp-strings have begun to cry out to the eagles."

That is the end, the last word. Like St. Patrick listening to Oisin's heathen words, we recognize a beautiful tale of infinite longing and insatiable desire for unearthly perfection caught from the dim abyss of time, and told again with all the sweetness and dreaming music that the enchanters grudged to common men when they took William Yeats from among us to delight them.

That much is hidden from us is the fault of our mortal ears and vision. These symbolic things— these parti-coloured dogs, and wise fools, and bearded forms upon the water, and woods of solid jewel-stone—they do not flash their inner meaning straight upon us, and without their inner meaning their purpose is obscure. Had we, too, been in fairyland, we know it would be different. There a poem like this will have an immense circulation, sung by Niam, graved in Ogham character by the elves, illuminated with the moonlit silver of a buff-tip's wing.

"A. E."

STARS in the purple of night, the pearly greys of morning, the ocean wind and the gush of rain, misty waters and the moors with mountains that change every moment from light to shadow—all that makes the outward face of Ireland so beautiful is found in " A. E.'s " verse. But it is not of the outward face he writes. That is a thing even visitors may sometimes see, but " A. E." tells of things that are hidden from the wise and prudent visitors and revealed only to the babes who have been nursed at the heart of the land.

For him the earth and sky and water are full of dim memories and ancient enchantment. He hears " a laughter in the diamond air, a music in the trembling grass." He hears " a tender voice calling ' Away.' " In the mountains there are doors by which poor mankind may pass into the Land of Youth. Where the scarlet cressets hang over the trembling pool at Ballylee, there is a cure for all things. Down through the purple air after sunset, the sacred Hazel Tree drops her ruddy berries, which are the Nuts of Knowledge. Upon the hills

the bright Hound of Ulla calls to battle, and into
the pool of midnight Lugh slings the Morning Star.
It is as the poet himself has sung in one of his books
("The Earth Breath")—

> "In the wet dusk, silver sweet,
>   Down the violet-scented ways,
> As I moved with quiet feet,
>   I was met by mighty days.

> . . . .

> "Where the hawthorn glimmered white,
>   Flashed the spear and fell the stroke—
> Ah, what faces pale and bright
>   Where the dazzling battle broke!"

Thus he stands ever "on the phantom verge of
things." To him, as he says in his volume of
"Homeward Songs," the rudest sod of the mother
earth is thrilled with fire of hidden day. To him
love flies as a white-winged star. His joy in all the
gods abides, and for him "the old enchantment
lingers in the honey-heart of earth."

With the same sense of enchantment and marvel
he approaches mankind. For if the mountains, that
sometimes look quite solid, can open doors into
fairyland, surely the spirit of man, which is not solid
at all, may reveal strange secrets. To this poet, as
to all the great spirits of the world, the outward
conditions of the spirit are of small concern, so long
as they do not rob the spirit of its natural glory. A

secret of Ireland's charm and power lies in that
poem among the " Homeward Songs "—

> " I pitied one whose tattered dress
>> Was patched, and stained with dust and rain ;
> He smiled on me ; I could not guess
>> The viewless spirit's vast domain.

> " He said, ' The royal robe I wear.
>> Trails all along the fields of light ;
> Its silent blue and silver bear
>> For gems the starry dust at night.

> " ' The breath of Joy unceasingly
>> Waves to and fro its folds starlit,
> And far beyond earth's misery
>> I live and breathe the joy of it.' "

This secret power over immensity that lurks, so
often obscured, in the heart of man, is, after all,
man's one distinction and cause for pride upon this
atom of the universe that we know, and the poet
shows us glimpses of it in many shapes and varieties,
often so fugitive that before we can realize them
they almost vanish. Sometimes it is " the old
protest, the old pity," of which Ireland's history has
been so bitterly full since the invasion. Sometimes
it speaks in the peacefulness but infinitude of a
summer night. Sometimes it is hidden in a vision
of ancient Babylon that rises from the look of a girl
in Ireland. And then, again, it is heard in the
tender voice of Dana, herself the mother of the
ancient gods, who now live on as the Sidhe—

"I am the heartbreak over fallen things,
The sudden gentleness that stays the blow,
And I am in the kiss that foemen give
Pausing in battle, and in the tears that fall
Over the vanquished foe, and in the highest,
Among the Danaan gods, I am the last
Council of mercy in their hearts where they
Mete justice from a thousand starry thrones."

In that same poem of " Dana " in " The Divine Vision and other Poems," there are other lines very characteristic of this poet—

" And fleeting ever from the passionate touch,
I shine afar, till men may not divine
Whether it is the stars or the beloved
They follow with rapt spirit."

All through his poems may be traced this delicate fear of contact, or of any near and earthly approach to the objects of the deepest affection and admiration. For the sake of the spiritual light—that ideal glory which might else be shattered—he would remain, as another poet has expressed it, " a stubborn exile from felicity," as felicity is generally counted among mankind, and to him love is the adoration of a star, such as would be blurred by the passionate touch that blunts the soul. So he sings—

" What a darkness would I gaze on when the day had passed
the west,
If my eyes were dazed and blinded by the whiteness of a
breast ;

Never through the diamond darkness could I hope to see
  afar
Where beyond the pearly rampart burned the purer
  Evening Star."

It is the same thought that we find in one of the
" Homeward Songs "—

  "Away ! the great life calls ; I leave
    For Beauty, Beauty's rarest flower ;
    For Truth, the lips that ne'er deceive ;
    For Love, I leave Love's haunted bower."

Such are the things of which this poet tells.
He is occupied with the phases of the soul, the
sorrows and joys of the spirit, which may sometimes
be suggested by external things and may correspond
in sympathy with the face of nature, but have no
necessary connection with events or any of the
visible things that happen and occupy so much of
our daily attention. He possesses the essential
power of vision, penetrating into those inward conditions of the spirit of which all things that appear
to exist are but the symbols. He stands, as we may
recall once more, "on the phantom verge of things."
Almost equally delicate in his perception of nature
with Mr. William Yeats, his interest seems almost
further removed from the visible things of this
world, and even more closely enwrapt in the spiritual
things that are called eternal. Without comparing
or contrasting these two poets who stand among the

leaders of that Irish revival which is the most remarkable spiritual event of our time, we may think
Ireland happy in possessing two such men.

Nor does it in the least surprise us that " A. E."
should be almost as well known in his own country
for his organization of co-operative agriculture as for
his poetry. It would be a pity indeed if the possession
of high powers unfitted a man to accomplish things
that even stupid people attempt with confidence.
To make the finer spirit's work surpass that of the
grosser by an immeasurable quality, only interest is
wanted. Certainly there is plenty of interest for a
poet in the contest for such a country's welfare, and
it would be a dull soul that could not discern the
eternal side in the effort to preserve such a people
for their own land.

Battles Long Ago

TO say that Lady Gregory's collection of the Irish legends called "Gods and Fighting Men," is worthy of her "Cuchulain of Muirthemne" is praise enough. As Mr. Yeats says in his preface, written words in praise of books like these must sound, in the ears of later generations—

"Like the foolish sound of church bells from the tower of a church when every pew is full."

She has here done for the cycles of the Danaan and the Fianna what she did in "Cuchulain" for the cycle of the Red Branch Knights. Searching the printed texts and manuscripts, consulting the best versions and renderings, she has herself translated and put together the most striking of the stories and poems, arranging them in some kind of order according to subject or cycle. But a continuous arrangement is, of course, impossible in legends that have come down to us after a passage through many various minds and long unwritten tradition, all disjointed and scattered like leaves that fall through darkness from an ancient tree. It is hard to tell where they belong, and impossible to fix their date.

The scholars have long believed that the stories of Finn and his followers come about the last of heathen poems, and the great dialogue of Finn's son Oisin with St. Patrick seemed a possible proof. But here is Mr. Yeats maintaining for all the Finn cycle a much earlier date—far away in the mists of time, long before Cuchulain and the Red Branch Knights. His evidence is entirely internal, but it is very strong, and the difference he finds between the mythical Fianna, to whom the gods were close, and the almost historic Kings of Cuchulain's time, is like the difference between Finn's home on the bare Hill of Allen, with its great spaces and windy light, and the green Hill of Tara, set among fat grazing lands.

Where the bards themselves have confused the ancient tales, and where tradition has passed unwritten from peasant to peasant through long centuries down to the last, while Christian scribes have added edification to their manuscripts, as to the tale of the Children of Lir, we need not look for any certainty. We can only say that in this present collection the stories of the Danaan seem to belong to a more childlike age, the marvels are more obvious and grotesque, and the legends come nearer the far-spread folk-lore of the world. Here we read of the fairy Manannan and the tricks he played, and how Miach, the skilful physician, from whose grave grew three hundred and sixty-five healing plants, once offered to fit a cat's eye into an empty socket—

" ' I would like that well,' said the young man. So Miach put the cat's eye in his head ; and he would as soon have been without it after, for when he wanted to sleep and take his rest, it is then the eye would start at the squeaking of the mice, or the flight of the birds, or the movement of the rushes ; and when he was wanting to watch an army or a gathering, it is then it was sure to be in a deep sleep."

Or take the broth that the race of Fomor made for Dagda when Lugh sent him to their camp to ask for an armistice—

" And then, to make sport of him, the Fomor made broth for him, for he had a great love of broth. So they filled the King's cauldron with four times twenty gallons of new milk, and the same of meal and fat, and they put in goats and sheep and pigs along with that, and boiled all together, and then they poured it all out into a great hole in the ground."

With an immense ladle Dagda had to eat it up on pain of death. So he tasted it and said, "If the broth tastes as well as the bits taste, this is good food." And he ate it all and scraped up what was left among the earth and gravel.

Even the earliest and most childlike tales are not all in this monstrous manner. They are full of brilliant descriptions of nature and of people, and from them we can build up a very gay picture of the early life in Ireland, or at least of what the people would have liked it to be at its best. Here

R

is Etain, as the High King of Ireland saw her,
before she was enchanted away by the Sidhe—

" He saw at the side of a well a woman, with a bright
comb of gold and silver, and she washing in a silver basin
with four golden birds on it, and little bright purple stones
set in the rim. A beautiful purple cloak she had, and silver
fringes to it, and a gold brooch ; and she had on a dress
of green silk with a long hood, embroidered in red gold,
and wonderful clasps of gold and silver on her breasts and
on her shoulder."

And here is one of the earliest of the many
descriptions of that land to which she was tempted
away—the Land of the Young, the Land of the
Ever Living, that plays so large a part in all Irish
tradition—

" The young never grow old there ; the fields and the
flowers are as pleasant to be looking at as the blackbird's
eggs ; warm, sweet, streams of mead and of wine flow
through that country ; there is no care and no sorrow in
any person ; we see others, but we ourselves are not seen.
Though the plains of Ireland are beautiful, it is little you
will think of them after our great plain ; though the ale of
Ireland is heady, the ale of the great country is still more
heady. It is ale and new milk I will give you for drink ;
it is feasting you will have with me there ; it is a crown
of gold you will have upon your hair, O beautiful woman ! "

But directly we come to the cycle of the Fianna,
which fills more than half the book, we rise to a
finer kind of legend and poetry. We approach what
Mr. Yeats calls the " songs of the sun," and the

sun, as the old symbolic writers tell us, brings with it not merely discipline, but joy. In this cycle we find the great epic passages of " The Battle of the White Strand," the story of Diarmuid and Grainne, and " The End of the Fianna." In these we have reached a fuller and nobler form of life, inspired by the high thoughts and passions of grown men and women, and, as is usual in all Irish poetry, the symbols of nature conspire with the moods of man. On the morning of the great fight upon the White Strand, we read :—

" Then the creatures of the high air answered to the battle, foretelling the destruction that would be done that day ; and the sea chattered of the losses, and the waves gave a heavy shout keening them, and the water-beasts roared to one another, and the woods trembled mourning the heroes, and the grey stones cried out at their deeds, and the wind sobbed telling them, and the earth shook, foretelling the slaughter, and the cries of the grey armies put a blue cloak over the sun, and the clouds were dark."

The tale of Diarmuid and Grainne is beautifully told, except that an inferior version is followed in one place. It is not that Grainne once plunged her dagger into her lover in rage ; that was natural enough to a woman who in answer to the question, " What is the best of jewels ? " replied, " A knife." But it is hard to believe that after that great lament over Diarmuid, when the boar killed him and Finn refused to save him, she could go quietly back and live with Finn upon the Hill of Allen. Of the heroes of the cycle it is hard to choose between Diarmuid the Beloved of Women, and Oisin, who went with golden Niam to dwell in the Land of the Young, and Osgar, the short-lived son of Oisin. The story of Osgar's death is thus told ; he is lying wounded on the field—

"And he put out his hand to Oisin, and Oisin took it, and gave out a very hard cry. And Osgar said, 'It is glad I am to see you safe, my father.' And Oisin had no answer to give him. And just then Caoilte came where they were, and he looked at Osgar. 'What way are you now, my darling?' he said. 'The way you would like me to be,' said Osgar."

In the fading away of the Fianna and the return of Oisin as a withered old man to find the land all changed and empty, the ancient poetry of Ireland reaches its height of pathos and tragedy. Nothing in the whole cycle surpasses the sorrow of Oisin's lamentation over the days that are gone ; and though the concluding scenes must have been written by a Christianized bard, his sympathy is always with this last of the heathen. At the very end of the dialogue with St. Patrick, it is Oisin says—

"My story is sorrowful. The sound of your voice is not pleasant to me. I will cry my fill, but not for God, but because Finn and the Fianna are not living."

Irish Plays of 1904

"WE always know when we are among our own people," said Mr. Yeats in his short speech, after the performance of *The King's Threshold*, and some critics who were present found the saying harsh and egoistical. "We admit we are but creeping Saxons," they said in effect, "but are we therefore incapable of appreciating great literature? Or is the perception of beauty the exclusive possession of the Celt?" I think they entirely misunderstand the poet's meaning. To me the saying, far from being egoistical, was singularly modest, and I took it to mean that it is an easy thing for an Irish poet to please his own people, just as success among strong personal friends is not hard to win. Mr. Yeats probably only intended to imply that the applause of the house may have been more kindly than deserved. That was his polite and modest way of putting it.

Yet in the other sense the saying would have been entirely just. It was easy to know that these Irish plays were given before an Irish audience—an audience, Irish in the main by birth, and sympathy.

This does not at all imply that the English people present were incapable of admiring the plays themselves as pieces of drama and literature. The interest was true enough and general enough to appeal to common humanity. But with how much deeper an emotion it appealed to those who had themselves sprung from the land where the scenes lay and who, in their blood and bone, felt their kinship with the figures that passed before them on the stage ! That is the meaning of nationality. Study Greek literature as we may, admire it beyond all limits of admiration as we may, how shall we ever feel in us the stir, the pride of possession, and the passionate affection, with which some Athenian witnessed a masterpiece from his city as he sat in an alien theatre across the sea ? The professors of Germany may elucidate Shakespeare for ever ; they will never know him like the men who were bred in Shakespeare's fields. Art is, after all, a national thing. Unless it draws its life from a deep and native soil, it is thin and bloodless. Nor can even the greatest artist ever hope to reveal the full beauty of his conception to any but his own people.

So with Mr. Yeats's play of *The King's Threshold*. A stranger could admire the simplicity of the whole conception, and the rigorous self-restraint of the acting. He could understand the obvious symbolism that beauty is the vitalizing principle of life, and that the State is rotten where poets are not at least on an equality with kings. He could glory in a poet's proud resolve rather to starve to death upon the bare steps of the palace than yield one jot of a poet's ancient right. He could appreciate the splendour of the lines upon the marriage of the stars and earth, and the noble voice and dignity with which Mr. F. J. Fay, as the poet "Seanchan," recited the final verses bidding the trumpets cry to the great race that is to come. But to the Irish people present the play stood for far more than this. It was full of strange lights and half-unconscious significance that they alone of all the audience had the right to feel or the power of perceiving. These kings and princesses and poets, these simple men from a hamlet by the seashore, were of their own blood. They were the people who once had lived in that land which has always been the object of such passionate sorrow and desire. After all, as some old hero said, no other land ever looks quite the same as one's country, and no other grave is like one's mother's. Or again, to take even the most obvious of the underlying interpretations of the symbolism, to an Irishman the proud starvation of the poet inevitably suggests the proud refusal of Ireland to be satisfied with anything less than her highest claim, and the King, who protests his love, and is only frightened about "the Crown" and its rights, is inevitably the hesitater, the trimmer, the "Unionist" and half-hearted friend, who wants to keep on calling himself a Liberal, but is driven bit by bit to coercion and the hangman's rope—

"I have been patient though I am a king,
And have the means to force you—but that's ended,
And I am but a king and you a subject.
Nobles and courtiers, bring the poets hither,
For you can have your way : I that was man
With a man's heart am now all king again."

Any one may see the parallel to the chilly Liberal who, under the excuse of "union," lets the Tories loose to their old coercion game. But to the Irish people such words come home with a poignancy of truth that no one of another race can suffer.

It was the same with the other plays. Perhaps, indeed, the intensity of national appeal was even more powerful in them. For they all dealt with scenes of actual peasant life, such as may still be witnessed in any of the really Irish parts of the country. All were remarkable, and, in spite of the exact similarity of the setting—so exact that the same scenery did for the four—the themes of all were so different that it is unnecessary to compare them or to put one above another. In *Riders to the Sea*, Mr. Synge has produced, not exactly a drama, but just a picture of a common crisis in the fisher life upon the west coast. One after another, the father and five sons have been drowned. The sixth goes out, his mother sees the omen of his death, his body is borne back upon a door, the women raise the lamentation, the mother has nothing now left to hope for or to fear, the coffin is to be made of nice white boards that were kept ready, though unhappily the nails had been forgotten.   That is all.   But in that brief and common scene, it is a miracle how much of the sadness and unnoticed pathos of Irish life the poet has gathered up, and how much of its unnoticed beauty, too.   The quiet "keening" of the two women who enter with the body, almost like ghosts, and keep up their monotony of lament through the rest of the dialogue, reaches the effect and dignity of an ancient chorus, so that the scene is transfigured into the world where mortal things are revealed under the image of eternity, and yet, all the time, the winds are howling around the walls of a poor Irish cabin, and the spray of the sea that swallows men is driving over the roof.

Broken Soil is by Padraic Colm, the latest and youngest of the Irish poets.   The theatrical critic would see much to find fault with in it.   The construction is amateurish, the passing to and fro through the same door becomes wearisome, the action, such as there is, seldom "comes to anything," and does not easily explain itself.   But its motives turn on some of the most powerful influences in the Irish nature—the love of a bit of land, the love of the open road, and the glory in skilful music.   It is the story of a daughter's devotion to her father's highest welfare—his artistic, or, if you will, his spiritual welfare—and it is told in delicate half-tones of humour and deep penetration into the nature of man. The quiet conclusion, when the four chief actors go out upon the road in pairs that will never return or meet again, and the friend sits down in absolute silence and gazes upon the deserted hearth, is one of the most impressive scenes in modern drama. But here, again, it is only Irish people to whom the real appeal is made, and to present such a play to an ordinary audience in a London theatre would have been little short of profanation.

Of the two farces, one of which cheerfully concluded the performance on each occasion, Mr. Yeats's *Pot of Broth* has been seen in London before, and is a most charming and natural piece of laughter over a rogue's cleverness. Mr. Synge's *In the Shadow of the Glen* has, perhaps, too serious a background for farce, and just touches the "problem" play, though the solution is absolutely right. But one cannot leave these farces without noticing the great skill with which Mr. W. G. Fay, in the chief comic parts, succeeded in avoiding even the shadow of resemblance to the vulgar clown who has so long been received as the typical Irishman upon the English stage.

" *The Dark Rosaleen* "

THERE is in Ireland an intention of putting up a memorial to Clarence Mangan, if only money enough can be collected. Whether, in the present state of art, a monument is of any advantage to the world, and whether poets who boast of work more durable than bronze had not better be satisfied with that kind of durability,—these are questions for artists. But there can be no doubt that, if any country ought to put up memorials to its poets, Ireland owes one to Clarence Mangan.

He was one of those peculiar plants of genius that produce only one perfect flower. He gave every promise of a poet, it is true. The sketch of him taken by Sir Frederick Burton as he lay dead in a Dublin hospital (whether he died of cholera or starvation is a nice point for discussion) shows a clear-cut face of great refinement and sensitiveness —a face like Schiller's, and having something in common with the faces of all lyric poets. We read of the brilliant and dreamy blue eyes, of the hair so abundant and so bright with gold before misery whitened it. His very dress was lyrical. The

accounts left by his few friends, Gavan Duffy
among them, all agree upon the steeple-crowned
hat with its immense brim, the tightly buttoned
coat that had once been a kind of drab, the little
blue cloak hardly reaching to the waist, the baggy
trousers made for some one better fed, and the
enormous umbrella which he kept tucked under
the cloak so that it looked like a bagpipe.

The apparition is poetic enough, and it seems
never to have varied, except that under opium and
drink it grew rather more spectral and dingy, till
suddenly it vanished underground. In external circumstance also, Mangan enjoyed every poetic advantage. He was born poor and remained so ; he was
well-read ; he was unmarried ; and he lived to forty-
six. Nor was his genius hindered by lethargy, or
indifference, or any over-scrupulous criticism of
himself. He was, on the contrary, rather peculiarly
fertile, and Mr. D. J. O'Donoghue, to whom we
owe the new edition of his writings, as well as the
biography published a few years ago, has discovered
over 800 of his poems that appeared in print. So
far from being barren, all his work shows the facility
and exuberance of a man who writes with ease, and
enjoys writing. There was nothing exiguous or
stinted about him, and yet, though he was quite
unaware of it himself, he reached high excellence
only once.

His devoted admirers, of whom I am one, may

bring up strong instances to the contrary. They may call to mind poems still familiar to the literary circle in Dublin, such as " O'Hussey's Ode to the Maguire," with its fine ending, so prophetic of De Wet—

" Hugh marched forth to the fight—I grieved to see him so
     depart ;
  And lo ! to-night he wanders frozen, rain-drenched, sad,
     betrayed—
  But the memory of the lime-white mansions his right hand
     hath laid
        In ashes warms the hero's heart ! "

Or they may call to mind the lament that, like the wood-pigeon, keeps asking, "Where, Oh, Kincora ? " or the Turkish song of " Karaman," or the Arabic " Howling Song of Al-Mohara," or the personal sorrow of " The Nameless One "—

  " Him grant a grave to, ye pitying noble,
      Deep in your bosoms !   There let him dwell !
   He, too, had tears for all souls in trouble,
      Here and in hell."

Or they may call to mind the regret for the days of the " Barmecides," so productive of Irish parody ; or the more genuine pathos of " Twenty Golden Years Ago," not unlike one of Béranger's smiling lamentations over lost youth—

  " Wifeless, friendless, flagonless, alone,
      Not quite bookless, though, unless I choose,
   Left with nought to do, except to groan,
      Not a soul to woo, except the Muse—

> O ! this, this is hard for *me* to bear,
> Me, who whilom lived so much *en haut*,
> Me, who broke hearts like chinaware
> Twenty golden years ago."

I will go further than other admirers, and add the "Lullaby," in which the rod of Moses, the diamond sceptre of Pan, and the Golden Fleece are mingled, in true Irish prodigality, with the glaive of O'Dunn, Diarmuid's sword, and Queen Eofa's jewels, as the best possible gifts to keep the baby quiet—

> "And Conal's unpierceable shirt of mail,
> And the shield of Nish, the prince of the Gael,
> These twain for thee, my babe, shall I win,
> With the flashing spears of Achilles and Finn,
> Each high as a pine ;
> O, hushaby, hushaby, child of mine !"

For such poems as these, Mangan would be remembered, as he is remembered, in any circle that made a special study of Ireland's literary spirit. Owing to that " Celtic Revival " which has been the one spiritual event of the last ten years, it is quite likely that some of them may appear in our recognized anthologies, and the name of Mangan will become familiar to the English child as one of poor, slovenly, drunken and incapable old Ireland's awful warnings.

By most people, even by admirers, the rest of Mangan's work will never be heard of again. Like all the Irish poets of his time, Mangan was much hampered, even in the use of words. They were writing a foreign language, and working on false models. For they had forgotten their own tongue, and the true power of English was hidden from them by the poetic artifice of their day. Take Mangan on his ordinary level, as in "The Geraldine's Daughter"—

"A beauty all stainless, a pearl of a maiden,
    Has plunged me in trouble, and wounded my heart;
With sorrow and gloom is my soul overladen,
    An anguish is there that will never depart."

Any Irishman of sixty years ago could have gone on like that to the other side of Godspeed. And to me —perhaps to me alone—there is a certain attraction about that kind of verse, the attraction of a genuine, though slightly faded, gentility. It reminds me of the modest little houses which are still seen in the sweetly mouldering suburbs of Dublin, bearing on their gate-posts of corroded stucco the titles of "Talavera," "Khyber Pass," or "Maharajpore," to recall the poor, battered, old hero who so trustfully served the foreign and dominant race, and inscribed those proud titles as his sufficient reward. Over such gate-posts, such verses, the sensibility of forty years ago would have shed a tear; and still the angels give them a smile of passing recognition.

But in "The Dark Rosaleen" we have no time to think about forms and words. Critics may tell

us there are echoes of a foreigner's English in it
still. That does not matter now. The dawdlers in
the suburbs of literature may drowse over such
things, if they please. They may debate with tepid
industry whether it was Mangan or Poe who first
invented the obvious characteristics of the metre.
In "The Dark Rosaleen" we have passed beyond
such things. We are borne away to a circle of
passion from which tasteful criticism is seen fluttering
with all its trumpery in the Paradise of Fools. The
winds and stars are round us, and "red lightning
lightens through the blood." We have passed into
a world of nobler vision, where we behold Ireland
incarnate again under the symbol of the Black Little
Rose—the *Roisin Dubh*—just as she once appeared
to Costello of Ballyhaunis, Red Hugh O'Donnell's
wandering singer, who first made that song of such
finely woven duplicity that the dull invaders never
could be quite sure whether it sang of treason or of
love. That early singer, in peril of his life, had
said—

"Oh, little rose,
Let there not be sorrow upon you for what has happened ;
The priests are coming over the waves, they are moving
    upon the sea.
Your pardon will come from the Pope of Rome in the
    East,
And Spanish wine will not be spared for my Dark Little
    Rose." [1]

[1] Slightly altered from Miss Guiney's translation of the Irish in her
"Study of Mangan" (1897).

It was from that verse that Mangan began—

> " O my Dark Rosaleen,
>   Do not sigh, do not weep !
> The priests are on the ocean green,
>   They march along the deep.
> There's wine from the royal Pope
>   Upon the ocean green ;
> And Spanish ale shall give you hope,
>   My Dark Rosaleen !
>   My own Rosaleen !
> Shall glad your heart, shall give you hope,
> Shall give you health, and help, and hope,
>   My Dark Rosaleen."

The Gaelic poet, whose name is a shadow, went on—

> "It was a long course over which I brought you from
>   yesterday to this day.
> Over mountains I went with you, and by sails across the
>   sea,
> The Erne I passed at a bound, though it was great with
>   flood,
> And there was music of strings on each side of me and
>   my *Roisin Dubh*."

Then Mangan sings—

> " Over hills and through dales
>   Have I roamed for your sake ;
> All yesterday I sailed with sails
>   On river and on lake.

S

> The Erne at its highest flood
>   I dashed across unseen,
> For there was lightning in my blood,
>   My Dark Rosaleen !
>   My own Rosaleen !
> Oh ! there was lightning in my blood,
> Red lightning lightened through my blood,
>   My Dark Rosaleen ! "

Intermingling the note of human love as though to lead the insensate enemy astray, Costello sings—

> " I would walk the dew with you and the desert of the
>   plains,
> In the hope to win love from you, or part of my desire.
> Sweet little mouth ! you promised you have love for me.
> Oh, she is the flower of Munster,
>   My Dark Little Rose ! "

But from a further depth of passion comes Mangan's cry, and the ruler must be dull indeed to miss the rebel's devotion here—

> " Over dews, over sands,
>   Will I fly for your weal :
> Your holy delicate white hands
>   Shall girdle me with steel."

The figure of a country rises like a religious vision before some soldier-saint in a ruined chapel of the forest or among Irish hills.   She is the Black Rose, the Secret Rose, holy as the Rose of Bethlehem. The poet is enamoured of her, as ancient citizens were enamoured of a city, but it is with a passion how much more tender and profound! She is no imperial state, standing in white-columned security over the seas which her fleets command ; but a shy and fugitive spirit, her beauty remains unseen by all except her worshippers. To strange eyes she looks a mournful and profitless thing. Full of sad memories, reviled and held up to derision, bound, tortured, and spat upon, called out to make sport with her wit, starved and driven through the earth, in turn half-strangled and cajoled as a pleasing strain for the nurseries of her tormentors, even to her lovers she takes the disguise of the Little Old Woman, the Kathleen na Houlihan, who sits uncomforted beside the world's highway, or crouches muttering over the peat-fires of her hearth, while under those worn rags, and under the disguise of that wrinkled skin, is hidden the pure form of that Dark Rose whose heart is the consecrated shrine of joy and sorrow—

> " All day long, in unrest,
>   To and fro do I move.
> The very soul within my breast
>   Is wasted for you, love !
> The heart in my bosom faints
>   To think of you, my queen,
> My life of life, my saint of saints,
>   My Dark Rosaleen !
>   My own Rosaleen !
> To hear your sweet and sad complaints,
> My life, my love, my saint of saints,
>   My Dark Rosaleen ! "

The poem first appeared in *The Nation*, the rebel newspaper of "Young Ireland." It was in 1846, perhaps the blackest year in the unbroken storm of Ireland's history since the Invasion. It may have been for that very reason that the "Dark Rosaleen" so far surpassed anything else that Mangan ever wrote. In the Introduction which John Mitchel, himself one of the greatest writers in *The Nation*, prefixed to the selection from Mangan's poems which was published ten years after his death, we find a sentence which, perhaps, explains why it is that this poem stands alone and apart, as something in an utterly different rank of excellence, from the rest of Mangan's work. Mitchel speaks first of the poet's poverty-stricken and miserable life, of his shy and sensitive nature; "modestly craving nothing in the world but celestial, glorified life, seraphic love, and a throne among the immortal gods;" and then, as an explanation of his entire neglect by English critics, he adds—

"Mangan was not only an Irishman,—not only an Irish papist,—not only an Irish papist rebel;—but throughout his whole literary life of twenty years he never deigned to attorn to English criticism, never published a line in any English periodical, or through any English bookseller, never seemed to be aware that there was a British public to please. He was a rebel politically, and a rebel intellectually and spiritually,—a rebel with his whole heart and soul against the whole British spirit of the age."

It was because Mangan found in " The Dark
Rosaleen " the fullest expression of that lifelong
rebellion that the poem is on quite a different level to
the rest of his work. In this alone he passed beyond
the ordinary themes and exercises of poetic talent—
the amorous addresses, the regrets for the past, the
translations from foreign tongues, over which he
wasted so much of his life. In nearly all his other
verses, he is untrue to himself and only plays the
common literary part. They are sometimes pretty,
sometimes " literature," and they are never anything
greater. But here he gathers up all the deepest
forces of his nature, to give us, just for this once,
the assurance of something more than a literary man.
In this cry of rebellion, prompted by a devotion like
a lover's, but more generous and of nobler mood, we
find at last the essential spirit of the poet. He was
a rebel with his whole heart and soul, says John
Mitchel. And his rebellion was inspired by the
vision of that sorrowful but endearing shape
which was his country—that beggar queen, starving
and glorified—that saint of saints, whose spirit
shone in gleams of opal. Like himself, she was
abused, ruined, and despised, but the light that
burned in her heart, burned in his as well. So
to her feet he brought his one great gift, and
there he uttered the words which expressed the
whole purpose of his scorned and distracted
life—

" But yet will I rear your throne
    Again in golden sheen ;
'Tis you shall reign, shall reign alone,
    My Dark Rosaleen !
    My own Rosaleen !
'Tis you shall have the golden throne,
'Tis you shall reign, and reign alone,
    My Dark Rosaleen !

.   .   .   .

The Judgment Hour must first be nigh
Ere you can fade, ere you can die,
    My Dark Rosaleen ! "

The " British spirit," against which Mangan was
a rebel, heart and soul, now calls this kind of passionate emotion " mere sentiment." That word " sentiment " has a history of some interest. It has seen
better days. Once it was used to describe all the
higher emotions ; and, indeed, it has much the same
meaning still, only that once it was used in praise,
and now it is invariably used in scorn. I have
watched the use of the word by our politicians,
leader-writers, and business men for the last ten
years, and I find that when they set something aside
as " mere sentiment," they really mean that it cannot
produce sixpence. The Bishop of Worcester, it is
true, lately protested that even " sentiment " cannot
always be safely disregarded, but he has not changed
the use of the word. To describe a thing as " mere
sentiment " is to assume it to be a natural object of
indifference or contempt ; and because no one was

ever sixpence the better for any of the higher
emotions, they are all included under the ban of the
same word.

Since the British spirit inevitably, therefore,
regards Mangan's passionate devotion as mere sentiment (for it never could produce sixpence), it is
worth while to discover what that spirit thinks the
natural and advantageous attitude towards the object
of his adoration would be. And let us take the
British spirit at its very best, as it is represented, for
instance, every week by a newspaper which is the
source of true culture to the thoughtful middle
classes, and is by them justly regarded as moderate
and reasonable in its judgments, besides being
capable of forgiveness towards our defeated opponents, and of sympathetic tenderness to the lower
animals. Such a newspaper certainly reveals the
British spirit in the most intellectual and benevolent
form, and it is in a spirit of exuberant benevolence
that it comments as follows upon some visit of the
King to Ireland—

" The Celtic Irish have never, owing to their want of
minerals, been able to share fully in the solid wealth of
Britain. Their island, though beautiful, has never attracted
the sportsman and the tourist, who every year carry so large
an income to the happy kingdom north of the Tweed, where
even the foibles of the people are just the foibles Englishmen
comprehend, and therefore forgive. . . .

" Much of all this it is impossible to alter, as impossible
as to change a pasture into a mine by merely desiring the

alteration; but something can be done which is worth doing.
The Court can visit Ireland. . . .

"Crowds will flock where the King has found it pleasant
to live, crowds whose wealth, if it does not exactly fertilize
as a new trade would, still produces variety, excitement, a
break in that melancholy monotony of which the Irishman
through all his literature is so apt to complain, as one of the
evils to which he is unjustly subjected." [1]

I wish the writer had explained exactly where in
Irish literature he found the Irishman so apt to
complain of that melancholy monotony. He says it
is everywhere, and I suppose he must have instances
by the score, all unknown to myself. But every one
will admit that in this passage we do find the British
spirit in benevolent, healthy, and fullblown perfection. By this spirit we are taught to see a country's
greatest happiness in coal-pits and iron foundries,
or, failing them, in rich visitors who will convert the
peasantry into gamekeepers, gillies, and caddies.
And, next to pits or parasites, this exponent of the
British spirit likes to see a Court, which he regards
as a thing to be desired, not from any devotion to a
noble line, or as an ideal of kingship, or as a symbol
of respect for some great ruler, but because it would
attract crowds "whose wealth, if it did not exactly
fertilize as a new trade would, still produces variety,
excitement, a break in that melancholy monotony "
—and so on. Variety, excitement, and a break—

[1] *The Spectator*, July 25, 1903.

these are the nearest approach to spiritual blessings
which this typical writer can imagine ; and even
these, though the products of wealth, are only a
kind of second-best, for the wealth of crowds attend-
ing the Court " does not exactly fertilize as a new
trade would."

We have come a long way from Mangan's
" Dark Rosaleen." We have come the immeasurable breadth of St. George's Channel. We have
crossed to the sphere of the British spirit, and, from
this English shore, the Dark Rosaleen certainly does
look a little unlucrative. She is less fertilizing
even than a Court, much less than a new trade.
No one was ever sixpence the better on her account,
except the police. How different things appear in
this happy land, where there is always a tourist or a
golfer in sight, if there is not a mine or a factory !
Here we see a real Court, and " crowds will flock
where the King has found it pleasant to live."
Here new trades fertilize on every side, and from
ten thousand chimneys the clouds drop fatness.
Here Comfort builds her shrine, and the law of the
Golden Mean prevails, banishing the falsehood of
extremes, and pointing to the example of our City
Fathers to prove the desirability of " broadening
slowly down." Here the wayward child of passionate devotion is suffocated at birth, and a " non-
committal attitude " succeeds to all the wealth of
prudential reservations. Here is the home of

common sense ; here the land of that British spirit against which Mangan was a rebel, heart and soul.

No one would deny the great advantages of such a spirit. To be sure, it is exposed to the drawback that, as a recent writer on English education has said, " common sense has never yet furnished motive powers for great objects," [1] and great objects have counted for something in the world's history. But, apart from great objects, the British spirit can always pride itself with justice upon its sanity, its caution, its accomplishment of definite purposes by small degrees, its substantial prosperity, and entire freedom from the inexplicable sorrows and passions that rock the soul. These are blessings that Mangan never knew ; they are beyond the reach of the Dark Rosaleen's worshippers, and probably he never realized how soothing is their influence upon the mind. Had he done so, he might have been tempted to abandon his rebellion, to make terms with the invader, and to seek the rewards which the British spirit undoubtedly can bestow upon its own children, and on all who follow its precepts.

That is the temptation to which we are all exposed. We all feel the attraction of the British spirit, and the blessings of Golden Mediocrity are very tangible. We like its definite aims, its general cheerfulness, its visible success. It is not always that we can remain, like Mangan, rebels against it, heart and

[1] Mrs. Emily Crawford in " Victoria, Queen and Ruler."

soul, and preserve an unshaken fealty to that Dark
Rosaleen who is the Ireland of the spirit. Yet we
know for certain that in all great enterprises—in the
arts, love, war, and every important affair of life—
the only part that counts is the part that exceeds
moderation ; the part that is sometimes called
" passion " and sometimes " sentiment," that dis-
regards worldly interests, has no personal aims, and
sets no limits to its desire, admiration, or rage.
" Prudence," said William Blake, " is a rich, ugly
old maid, courted by Incapacity," and all who would
remain true, like Mangan, to the Dark Queen of
the soul must leave those wooers to the mediocre
progeny likely to fill their well-appointed nurseries,
while they themselves pursue the road into the
austere land of excess. An austere land we may
call it, for passion burns up all pretty adornments and
signs of ease, so that, where she passes, the country
is bare as a desert. But through it the adventurous
road leads to the world's end, where laws shrivel up,
and duty vanishes like an ineffectual ghost.

Men of any nation may thus become champions
of the Dark Rose. For every soul is a disunited
Kingdom of Great Britain and Ireland, nor is
spiritual success to be won except by persistent
rebellion against that predominant partner, which is
the commonplace.

Past and Present

I T is impossible to pass without welcome a new edition of Jocelin of Brakelond. For two shillings you may now get the whole chronicle in a little volume in "The King's Classics." It is an admirable translation, with all necessary guides in the way of preface, notes, historical explanations, table of dates, and index, to say nothing of a portrait of Abbot Samson himself as he appears on his own seal, holding his crozier and book, and vested in amice, alb, tunic, dalmatic, chasuble, rationale, and mitre. The whole has been arranged, edited, and annotated by Sir Ernest Clarke, and if any wish for an imaginative exercise in history or in the higher economics, here is the book he should obtain and read at leisure side by side with Carlyle's "Past and Present," to which this very chronicle formed the text and owes its widest fame.

We now stand at a crisis of our country's history very similar to the time when, exactly sixty years ago, Carlyle issued that volcanic little book, the first of the pamphlets by which he so profoundly influenced and even changed the aspect of economic theory and social aims in England. Almost the same problems are before us now. They concern more people, they appear rather larger and more complicated. The difficulties of the past always seem comparatively simple, for in thinking of them we omit the elements of fear and uncertainty, and as a rule we can see their issue, which appears inevitable because it has happened. Yet to our grandfathers of sixty years ago the problems of life were quite as difficult as our own, and they were rather peculiarly the same. So it is at a very opportune moment that Sir Ernest Clarke brings out his edition and recalls to us the chronicle in which Carlyle found so much ensample, warning, and guidance for his generation.

The suddenness of Jocelyn's story is astonishing. There is nothing to compare with it but the rise and fall of the curtain in a theatre. There the interval between the entrance and exit is filled with imaginary inventions, but in Jocelin it is filled with actual things—with sights and sounds that were seen and heard upon the solid world. Time is rent, and across seven centuries we gain a glimpse of scenes so vivid that they might be happening still. In a flash the ages have vanished that brought the printing-press and gunpowder and Greek ; that overturned the ancient Church, and broke the royal power ; that bore the steam-engine, and covered the island with furnaces and ash-heaps, and set ten men to stand where one stood before, and revealed the Americas and Antipodes, and gave us Empires and all those wars. In a flash we see the Abbey of St. Edmund still a-building, and old Hugh the Abbot going blind and obviously nearing his latter end. It is a famous Abbey and a rich ; it contains the actual body, head and all, of a martyr-saint as yet without rival on that side of England ; for Thomas of Canterbury was but three years dead, and reverence to him was still a dubious matter considering the temper of Henry, the energetic, orderly, but distinctly irascible King, who had not yet done his penance at the tomb.

But in spite of these advantages, the Abbey is in a confused and unhappy state, its finances all in chaos, its debts uncertain and increasing, the monks making their own seals and borrowing for their own advantage, Jews becoming so impudent on the strength of their claims that they run in and out of the monastery as they please, shelter their wives and children there in war-time, and actually ramble about the altars and round the shrine while High Mass is being said. Life is allowed to slide along carelessly from day to day, no order kept, no decency observed, and nothing said. Abbot and cellarer are at perpetual feud over the payment for the knights, legates, pilgrims, and other guests who flock to the shrine and demand hospitality as their right. The Abbey's rentals, hidages, fodder corn, hen-rents, and other dues are allowed to slip or shamefully diverted into other hands. There are whispers that the reputation of some of the monks is not untarnished : *tacenda quædam*, we read of—" unmentionable things," scandalous to the great communion of Benedict. And outside the walls are endless difficulties about wards and feudal rights, about clerks and seculars, about King and Pope, and wars with France and Flanders, and rebellions of the King's sons ; and all the time the trumpets blare for the Crusade. Here are " problems " enough calling for a serious man's deliberation and settlement, and by the brief glimpse given us in the forty pages or so of manuscript left by a gossiping monk and preserved by mere good luck when every other treasure of the shrine is lost, we are able as in no other case to summon up before us the real life which those problems concerned—the life of an age that till quite lately was called indifferently Mediæval or Dark. From no constitutional history, from no record of kings and wars and law-giving, and from no historical romance do we get a picture of early English life to be compared for truth and interest with the scenes that but for those few leaves in monkish Latin would have vanished from us as utterly as though they had never been. It is, as Carlyle says—

"Behold, therefore, this England of the year 1200 (Jocelin, in fact, begins his story in 1173) was no chimerical vacuity or dreamland, peopled with mere vaporous Fantasms, Rymer's Fœdera, and Doctrines of the Constitution ; but a green, solid place that grew corn and several other things. The sun shone on it ; the vicissitude of seasons and human fortunes. Cloth was woven and worn ; ditches were dug, furrow-fields ploughed, and houses built. Day by day all men and cattle rose to labour, and night by night returned home weary to their several lairs. In wondrous Dualism, then as now, lived nations of breathing men ; alternating, in all ways, between light and dark, between joy and sorrow, between rest and toil—between hope, hope reaching high as Heaven, and fear deep as very Hell."

There lies the value of the book ; it brings mankind into history, and delivers us from the lists, names, and dates and documents with which the learned are always trying to put us off. What would we not give for a similar glimpse into life at one of the fortress castles—say at Bamborough, or Naworth, or Harlech, or Corfe ! In Jocelin's story three kings appear and vanish. We see Henry II., and twice he swears " by the very eyes of God ; " we see the Lion-Heart, furiously raging at an imagined wrong, and appeased like a boy by the gift of a few nice dogs ; and we see John, entertained at the Abbey with enormous expense, and making no offering but thirteen pence for a Mass, and a silken cloth, which his servants had borrowed from the sacrist and never paid for. We would give something for the story of any of those kings told as Jocelin could have told it had he lived with one of them day and night for six years as he lived with Abbot Samson. And yet we would not change, for any one may get some knowledge of a king, but of Abbot Samson there is not a human being now living (except the antiquaries) who would have heard a single word without Jocelin's help.

England has not been rich in saints. The Celts have had their share ; the early Saxon Church produced a few ; but since the national character took its form, it has hardly produced one saint that counts. Nearly all the great saints have sprung from Italy, France, or Spain. Our race has seldom shown itself capable of the simplicity, meditation, prayerfulness, and visionary rapture that go to sanctitude. We have had plenty of very good men, but almost without exception they have followed a life of action, and have been distinguished for war, business, organization, discovery, or some other form of practical work.

So it is with Abbot Samson ; we find in him no more than the typical Englishman at his best. He was a religious man certainly. It did not occur to him, it hardly occurred to any one, to question the doctrines of the Church. He held his main principles as absolute and eternal truths, only doubted by Jews and the heathen, for whom hell was ready. His profound reverence at the opening of St. Edmund's coffin is the true nature of worship. No charge of sin, excess, or even indulgence is ever

T

brought against him. His manner of life was rigorous and clean. But for all that he was not of the stuff that saints are made of. Jocelin admits it : " The Abbot preferred an active life to one of contemplation," he says, "and rather commended good officials than good monks." He was himself, in fact, a model official of the English type. Capable of long obedience, and careless of external signs of power, he was still so firm of purpose that the old Abbot Hugh complained he was the only man he could not bend. We hear first of his skill in building, his arrangement of the sacred pictures, and his composition of verses to explain them. He was continually building and restoring the Abbey's possessions, clearing land, enclosing parks for the chase, and breeding dogs, though he took no part in sport. His first endeavour as Abbot· was to restore the monastery's finance ; he could never rest, we are told, till he knew the full extent of the debts. He was zealous for the Abbey's wealth, purchasing valuable manors (for which he offered half price first), seldom remitting dues, checking tyranny against the poor, but insisting on his uttermost rights against the citizens of London in the matter of his fair and their claim to carry Yarmouth herrings through his demesnes. He was continually involved in trouble with his cellarer, his sacrist, his hospitaller, his purveyors, and even his dean, who ran up a mill without leave and had to pull it down with extraordinary rapidity. In hopes of stopping up the sink of debt, he drove the Jews out of Bury altogether. Whenever he went abroad, he returned with some worthy gift for the shrine—a fine copy of the Gospels, a golden cross, a chasuble, a mitre, or sandals, and a silver crozier. In the Courts, bribery was powerless over him.

One minute touch of character is preserved in his gift of the manor of Thorpe to an English villein, " whose honesty he trusted the more as he was a good husbandman and could not speak French." So Bismarck said he never trusted an Englishman who spoke French well. For himself, Samson, " though indifferent to style," could be eloquent in French or Latin, but always preached in English, " of the Norfolk dialect." His aspect was acute and penetrating ; he rarely smiled ; he worked without ceasing, though he was fond of going off to one of his manors, because he found his temper so much better there than at home. Among his monks, as some had foretold at his election, he did at times " rage like a wolf." Slackness, dishonesty, luxury, or disobedience would kindle such a flame within him that his heart surged and he nearly choked with rage. At such times he would absent himself to calm his anger, and on return would offer reconciliation (always retaining his own way) and kiss again in copious tears.

Except for those tears, which our public schools

have suppressed, it is a regularly English type of character, and on the whole the best type our country produces in any abundance. Carlyle did not sufficiently recognize that the kind of man is still not uncommon. He chose examples of the other types he saw around him, and compared them with Abbot Samson, very much to their disadvantage. In the midst of vague theorising and talk about first principles, economic laws, and the action of the State, his object was to show the supreme value of the person, the individual character, the man apart from the averages of statistics or legislation. That value still exists ; it is at least as powerful now as sixty years ago. On the leaven of such character as Samson's, diffused throughout all classes, the strength and beauty of the country and the empire depend far more than upon markets, gold-mines, tariff laws, and unexampled prosperity. And if we are inclined to think that the race is still richer in this kind of leaven than Carlyle himself supposed— well, it is so much the better for us all. For the type is capable of stern endurance and noble activity ; it is possessed by a passion for justice, and against all the assaults of corruption it stands above suspicion.

The White Rose

" Ye Jacobites by name, give an ear, give an ear !
Ye Jacobites by name, give an ear ! "

FOR here, in his " Prince Charles Edward,"
Mr. Andrew Lang tells the story of
your darling. Here is revealed, as
though in life, the fount and origin of
those wild hopes, that glorifying recklessness of
devotion, and all those tears. In this man's
life, the smouldering romance which had flickered
from time to time amid the unemotional common-
sense of our country's history, leapt up into one
bright flame, and then fell extinguished, as it seems,
for ever. This is the nearest point to which the
spirit of romance can reach back through time for
the delicate food which it loves. It is now more
than a century and a half away from us, but still it
is the nearest point. To this our writers of romance,
who have not the wit or the patience to discern the
spiritual beauty underlying the human life even of
our own age, still naturally turn. But, what is far
more significant, the true poets of romance, whose
sense creates its own beauty in whatever they touch,
still turn to it too.

It has become the romantic inheritance of the

race.   We imbibe its spirit from childhood's stories, which are as deeply intermingled with our blood as the Bible.   We have heard its voice in all the brave, sad songs which have wailed and rung across the Border.   What poets except renegades of the soul, time-serving officials paid for poetry in terms of cash and sherry, have ever sung the Hanoverian dynasty ?   It seems that the name of George choked their singing.   Or what Germanised maker of odes has written a line or sung one note to compare to such lines and music as " Cam' ye by Athol ? " or "As he came marching up the street," or " And will ye no come again ? " or " It was a' for our rightfu' King " ?   If not by name, it seems we are all Jacobites at heart, or once were so in some bright and generous period of our now encumbered lives.

Nor is it only the poets and romancers who have thrown this glamour around the fallen House.   By nature we are all rebels fighting for " our righfu' King " against a Hanoverian dynasty of common-place.   Our hearts are the natural home of all lost causes, and it is but as symbols of that perennial struggle that we love the memory of every high-souled gentleman and every shaggy savage from the hills, who died for " Charlie."

> "Their winding-sheet the bluidy clay,
>   Their graves are growing green to see :
> And by them lies the dearest lad
>   That ever blest a woman's ee ! "

It is all very long ago, but that makes no difference to the pathetic radiance which surrounds their names or their nameless oblivion. There is a deeper significance in our love for the story than even Mr. Lang in the following passage has expressed—

"Scott speaks of a gentleman of the name of Stuart, who, in 1788, was seen in mourning, and was asked for what relations he wore it. ' For my poor chief,' he answered ; and it is in the spirit of this reply, and with this pardoning pity, that all who have a heart to care for a ruined enterprise, and a brave man undone, must think of the Prince. He failed utterly, failed before God and man and his own soul, but, if he failed greatly, he had greatly endeavoured. Charles is loved for his forlorn hope ; for his desperate resolve ; for the reckless daring, the winning charm that once were his ; for bright hair and brown eyes ; above all, as the centre and inspirer of old chivalrous loyalty, as one who would have brought back a lost age, an impossible realm of dreams."

The sad story, so beautiful in spite of its wretched end, begins with the picture of a bright-eyed and high-spirited child, who could be happy and childlike even among the melancholy etiquette of an exiled Court. One of his little letters, written when he was about eight, is given by Mr. Lang in facsimile from the Windsor collections—

"DEAR PAPA,—

"I thank you mightily for your kind letter. I shall strive to obey you in all things. I will be very dutifull to mamma, and not jump too near her. I shall be much obliged to the Cardinal for his animals. I long to see you soon and in good health. I am, dear papa, your most dutifull and affectionate son,

"CHARLES P."

This letter must have been supervised. At all events, when he grew up, the Prince never spelt so well again. He was nothing of a student or lover of books, but in youth a good golfer, and fond of hunting. Contrary to the general opinion, it is certain that he was never much given to women, and to this indifference Mr. Lang attributes his extreme popularity among them. At all events, they gave him all that women can give, whether in the way of delight, devoted aid, mockery, or interminable trouble. His proper place was not in courts or salons or ladies' ante-rooms, but with the clans upon the heather. There he was at his best, cheerful, brave, and generous of heart. He was barely fifteen months in Scotland altogether, but into that brief space all his real life was crowded. Mr. Lang devotes more than half the book to those fateful months, and he might perhaps have given them a higher proportion still. For all the rest is but a preparation or a pitiable decline, and it is for that short-lived flower of his existence alone that the man is valued.

Charles, like most men, required opportunity before he could show the real stuff that was in him.

Without that one kindling opportunity he would have passed through life as a pleasant country gentleman, unnoticed and unsung. But given health, danger, adventurous crises, and the open-air life of camps and battles—given all, in fact, that men naturally love, and so seldom get—he developed qualities surpassing anything that might have been expected from his ordinary nature. The same gift of rising with the opportunity to higher powers was seen to some extent in all the Stuarts ; certainly in Charles I., and pre-eminently in Mary of Scots, from whom, however, anything astonishing might be looked for. So it was with Charles when he stood at the head of his poor little team of High-landers—two thousand five hundred in all, many of them armed with scythes. His military judg-ment, often overborne, was generally right. To his enemies he was tolerant and chivalrous, perhaps beyond the duty of warfare, but one only admires him the more for that. From first to last he showed the good manners, the good taste, and the uncom-plaining endurance of a gentle mind.

" ' His body was made for war,' says Lord Elcho, and he did not spare it ; usually sleeping in his boots. He marched at the head of the clans. ' People thought it was only for a mile or two, to encourage the soldiers at the beginning, and were surprised to see him continue all day, but it was the same every day during the whole expedition ; in dirty lanes and deep snow he took his chance with the com-mon men, and would seldom be prevailed upon to get on horseback and cross a river. It's not to be imagined how much this manner of bringing himself down to a level with the men, and his affable behaviour to the meanest of them, endeared him to the army. . . .' So writes Maxwell of Kirkconnel, who was with the army, and is a thoroughly trustworthy witness."

Mr. Lang tells the story of the rising itself with fine strength and lucidity. Hardly once—we think only once—does he allow the romance of the subject to carry him away. In his treatment he is as accurate as sympathetic. But his sympathy is strong, and he sees where the true pathos of the event lies, in the uncalculating devotion of a few rough mountaineers who had nothing to gain.

" As the most remote and inaccessible of the Celts, they were most under the rule of Celtic ideas, fidelity to the chief and to the clan. Mainly pastoral in their life, and cultivating but a little grain, far from towns, and dwelling in little clachans, or villages, beside their scanty oatfields, they had much more of leisure than of employment. In their smoky huts, or in mountain shielings, poor and proud, their vigour was not undermined, or cramped, by labour. They were all sportsmen and gentlemen, except the most servile septs, who were not of kin to the chief. These were but half-armed, and their uncouth aspect amazed the Lowlanders. The spirit of the others was nurtured on ancient tales of war and Ossianic ballads. They thus formed an admirable militia, trained to the gun in sport, to the sword in private quarrel, and to long and secret marches, in the course of cattle-stealing."

So the story of their high endeavour goes on, from the landing at Moidart, to the occupation of Edinburgh, the wild charge at Prestonpans, the march to Carlisle, and on to Manchester, the advance to Derby, the fatal hesitation on the part of the Prince's advisers, and the reluctant retreat, of which, as Mr. Lang says, no young and generous heart has ever read without a pang. One passage in that cold and gloomy retirement (it was in December) shows the advantage of the kilt as a part of a soldier's uniform.

"The Highlanders, shoulder to shoulder, forded Esk in red spate, a hundred men abreast. 'The water was big and took most of the men breast high.' Lord George (Murray) was in his philabeg. 'Some ladies had passed the water on horseback, just before us; but had they looked back, they could have seen nothing, the water was so big. The pipes began to play as soon as we had passed, and the men all danced reels, which in a moment dried them, for they held the tails of their short coats in their hands in passing the river, so when their thighs were dry all was right.'"

The account of the little-known engagement at Falkirk is an excellent example of Mr. Lang's descriptive style, and so indeed is the larger theme of the ill-considered night attack and overwhelming disaster at Culloden—"Drumossie moor, Drumossie day." But the chapter called "In the Heather," with its long-loved stories of disguises and escapes and incorruptible loyalty, and with Flora Macdonald to crown them all, is the part to which lovers of romance will chiefly turn.

Then sorrow comes, not in the mere loss of crown and fortune and state, but in the loss of soul. We can, indeed, hardly endure to follow the decline and extinction of so clement and quick-hearted a nature ; but here we may now read, if we will, the full history of those unhappy years ; how the hero of the Forty-five slunk from Court to Court, sometimes disappearing for years, sometimes accompanied by an unloved mistress and child, sometimes by an unloving and sarcastic wife, who in the end left him for Alfieri, and probably did right. We may read how he wrote to a friend, " My heart is broke enough, without that you should finish it ; " how he quarrelled with his brother and refused to see his father again ; how he cadged for money, and sank ever deeper into the degradation of drink. But for all the lamentable and sordid history we cannot do better than quote Mr. Lang's own words—

" There is no unhappier fate, no more cruel catastrophe. What he should have done after 1746, it is not easy to decide. . . . The only alternative of which he could conceive was a life of lurking, where his active spirit and body were first devoured by indolence, and then ruined by the desperate resource familiar to extreme poverty and extreme despair. . . . A posthumous loyalty still cherishes a belief in ' exaggeration ' by enemies. We are told that ' it was an age tolerant of hard drinking.' It was not tolerant of solitary and shameful excesses ; and the charges rest, not on the slanders of enemies, but on the remonstrances of broken-hearted friends.   About such a character and such a life as Charles's had become, silence is the best record."

Mr. Lang has had the advantage of consulting the full collection of Stuart papers at Windsor, hitherto unpublished.   He has carried out the whole work with the care and industry of a historian, and our only complaint is that he has at times, especially towards the end, crowded his facts too closely together.   He has been unwilling to omit anything, and yet the space was limited.   It is the same fault as in his "History of Scotland."   The wood is too thick.   Perhaps he was afraid of omitting something which might at some time be useful to somebody. Perhaps he was afraid of being taken for "only a man of letters."   The method, at all events, makes parts of the book difficult and uninteresting.   But still stranger to us are two or three instances of peculiar reserve, as though secrets of one hundred and fifty years ago might work mischief still.   "To quote (certain letters) at this distance of time," he says, "and to name the writers may well seem invidious."   But when may they be quoted if not at this distance of time?   Or what are the "many good reasons" which Mr. Lang says forbid a further examination of two shadowy claims to Stuart descent in recent times?   Only the inanity of the subject, one would think.

De Wet

IN the frontispiece to De Wet's "Three Years' War," an autotype from Mr. Sargent's crayon drawing shows us the very man, as I first saw him during the war. It is the strong, rough face of one whose fathers have been for generations in close contact with the earth. The broad, low forehead, the nose broad and straight, the mouth tightly closed and long, the careless hair and beard, the heavy eyebrows—all of these are the common possessions of a good farmer stock. But under the eyelids, which droop markedly at the corners, are the keen, straight eyes which illumine the whole with the kind of genius that never knows hesitation or despair, and is never utterly at a loss ; and in the curved lines from the nostrils to the corners of the mouth lie the restrained humour of one whose fearlessness and self-confidence are founded on a shrewd estimate of his own and other people's value —an estimate which long experience of danger and crisis has confirmed.

The book tells the same story. We find in it a character that would have succeeded in any career which demands untiring energy, quick decision, and

an unerring grasp of the situation. Yet quite devoid,
it seems, of ambition ; for in the record of his
successes there is not a note of personal elation, and
he sometimes naïvely wonders that he could have
been so fortunate. It is strange to think that but
for the war he would have remained a Free State
farmer, with perhaps a seat in the Bloemfontein
Parliament, and the world would have known
nothing of one of its most brilliant soldiers and
leaders of men. When the call to action came he
took service as an ordinary burgher with his fellows,
and the honours which naturally followed him were
taken only as further opportunity in the great issues
of time. Outwardly so calm and reticent, we feel
throughout the book how ready he was to kindle
into one blaze of indignation at the sight of incapacity, cowardice, or treachery. " How angry I
was ! " he exclaims now and again, and we can
imagine how that flame of wrath shrivelled up its
object.

Stupidity and dull confusion were bad enough ;
we see how often they drove his quick mind almost
to distraction. But those he could forgive if they
were accompanied by honesty and pluck. He fully
realized, for instance, the immense disaster of obsti-
nate old Cronje's surrender at Paardeberg. But for
himself, one knows, the resistance would have collapsed a few weeks after that, instead of two years
later. " The effect of that blow," he says, " was

apparent to the very end of the war." Yet of the old general himself, even when giving an astounding instance of his blindness, he speaks "with the highest honour as a hero incapable of fear." And again—

"The world will honour that great general and his brave burghers ; and if I presume to criticise his conduct on this occasion, it is only because I believe that he ought to have sacrificed his own ideas for the good of the nation, and that he should not have been courageous at the expense of his country's independence, to which he was as fiercely attached as I."

On Prinsloo's surrender to General Hunter his language is very different—

"What, then, is to be our judgment on this act of Prinsloo and of the other chief officers in command of our forces behind the Roodebergen ?   That it was nothing short of an act of murder committed on the Government, the country, and the nation to surrender three thousand men in such a way.   Even the burghers themselves cannot be held to have been altogether without guilt, though they can justly plead that they were only obeying orders.   The sequel to Prinsloo's surrender was on a par with it.   A large number of burghers from Harrismith and a small part of the Vrede commando, although they had already made good their escape, rode quietly from their farms into Harrismith and there surrendered to General Sir Hector Macdonald.   One could gnash one's teeth to think that a nation should so readily rush to its ruin."

A like passion of indignation, even more restrained, is seen when he is driven to remember the sufferings of the women and children during the war. It bursts out, and is at once suppressed with the apology : "I had to unburden my heart." But there is no fire like a latent fire, and we should like to have been present that day when he "was very polite, but very determined" in informing his burghers that no waggons were allowed on commando henceforth, and next morning found that the owners were not only cleaving to their waggons, but were driving off home with them, leaving him with hardly a man at a moment of extreme crisis. "How angry I was!" he cries again ; and we can well imagine the scene.

It is wonderful what a clear and connected narrative he makes out of excursions and alarms that to us often seemed so devious or purposeless. Devious they generally were, but purposeless never. Hardly had one plan prospered or failed than he threw himself impetuously into another. Probably throughout those three years there was no living man who so seldom sat down to rest and recover. The thing he had just accomplished seemed nothing to the next thing he was going to do. Perhaps the history of his career would be best linked up by the order of his seven greatest exploits—the tragedy at Nicholson's Nek, when he captured over 800 of two famous British battalions on the nineteenth day of the war ; the capture of Lord Roberts's enormous convoy of food and material on the Riet River ; the destruction of Broadwood's force at Sanna's

U

Post ; the capture of 470 of the Royal Irish Rifles
at Reddersburg immediately afterwards ; the destruction of the railway and winter stores at Roodeval
just as Lord Roberts was needing everything for
Pretoria ; the capture of Dewetsdorp, the place named
after his father ; and the annihilation of the Yeomanry
camp at Tweefontein, near Harrismith, in the darkness of a Christmas morning.

Those are the guiding exploits, and the story of
each is told with vigorous simplicity and absolute
clearness. But in the intervals between these exploits
come the long weeks of rapid movement, of failure,
of hiding, and almost incredible escapes. We find
him rushing round from Ladysmith, much against his
will, to take up his first high command under Cronje
in the west, and thus just missing Colenso and other
battles of that black week. We see him flickering
round Lord Roberts's advance, trying to save old
Cronje, trying to stem the mad flight from Poplar
Grove. He sends his burghers home to recover
their spirits ; he brings them dashing in again upon
the English flank and rear ; he fails at Wepener,
though stimulated by his hatred of South African
colonial troops ; he hears of his brother Piet's
success against Colonel Spragge at Lindley ; he
begins his long series of interruptions to the railway
on which the very existence of the army in Pretoria
depended ; he only just misses the capture of Lord
Kitchener himself ; he crosses the Vaal, and taking

a circuit to the west penetrates to the Zoutpansberg
in the northern Transvaal ; he swings back again,
leading his horses over the Magaliesberg precipices
where no path was ; he is present at the terrible
scene at Bothaville, when Colonel Le Gallais,
" without doubt one of the bravest English officers I
have ever met," came charging over the open upon
the sleeping bivouac ; he sweeps south through the
country of his boyhood, and plunges through the
Orange River into Cape Colony ; driven back by
rain and hunger, he finds himself in his very tightest
corner, with the flooded river in front and " my dear
old friend Sir Charles Knox " behind ; he discovers
the one ford just practicable, and is away over his
own country, galloping his men and his President
straight through the enemy's converging lines,
between the guns of their two forts on Springhaans-
nek ; he makes his second attempt upon Cape
Colony, is again foiled by floods, and only escapes
by doubling sharp round and passing his pursuers
in the night ; for months he flits about the Orange
Colony, cutting the railway, laying his plans for
Tweefontein, defying the blockhouses—" the policy
of the blockhead," he impolitely calls them, breaking
through their lines sometimes—not by driving cattle
at them, he carefully explains ; there was no need of
that—courage and cutters were the only things he
used. That is in outline the course of " ole man
De Wet," as our soldiers loved to call him.

This epic of adventure and warfare is all told with a simplicity which is, perhaps, even more marked in the original Dutch. (The translation, by the way, is admirable, except for a few mistakes, such as a frequent use of "off-saddle" where obviously "up-saddle" is required.) The style bears out the General's expressed purpose of telling, not indeed the whole truth about the war, but at all events nothing but the truth. But this impression of quiet simplicity can, of course, be gained only from the book as a whole, and we will take one or two quotations rather from passages where the simple narrative style is just broken. De Wet fixes to Nicholson's Nek a story which we have wrongly heard told of Spion Kop—

"A Jew came up to a burgher who was lying behind a stone, on a piece of ground where boulders were scarce. 'Sell me that stone for half-a-crown,' whined the Jew. 'Loop!' the Boer cried, 'I want it myself.' 'I will give you fifteen shillings,' insisted the Jew."

But even in a rising market like that, the burgher would not sell. One little criticism on Buller is of interest now—

"This I will say, that whatever his own people have to say to his discredit, Sir Redvers Buller had to operate against stronger positions than any other English general in South Africa."

On his own astonishing escapes, we have this pathetic confession—

" To flee—what could be more bitter than that ? Ah ! many a time when I was forced to yield to the enemy, I felt so degraded that I could scarcely look a child in the face ! Did I call myself a man ? I asked myself, and if so, why did I run away ? No one can guess the horror which overcame me when I had to retreat, or to order others to do so —there ! I have poured out my whole soul. If I did fly, it was because one man cannot stand against twelve."

Or we may take his final generous tribute to his President, who, contrary to general expectation, had endured at his side every peril and hardship of the campaign—

" President Steyn was a statesman, in the best sense of the word. He had gained the respect and even the affection of us all. Of him, if of any man, it may be said that he never swerved from his duty to his country. No task was too great for him, no burden too heavy, if thereby he could serve his people. Whatever hardships he had endured, he had never been known to complain—he would endure anything for us. He had fought in our cause until he could fight no longer, until sickness laid him low : and he was worn out, and weak as a child. Weak, did I say ? Yes ! but only in the body—his mind was still as strong, as brave, as clear as ever."

Then follows an account of the negotiations, an almost verbatim report of the main conferences being given in the appendix. The whole proceedings are of the greatest interest, and up to the very last we see De Wet urging the delegates to maintain the struggle for independence. Not that he ever expected final victory. As he says in one place—

"We knew, I need scarcely say, that humanly speaking ultimate victory for us was out of the question—that had been clear from the very beginning. . . . Yet we had always felt that no one is worthy of the name of man who is not ready to vindicate the right, be the odds what they may."

The whole book is a noble addition to the epic of South Africa. In every way it is worthy of the soldier of instinctive genius, who was the Stonewall Jackson of the war. It is interesting to conjecture what the future of such a man may be. He promises us a book on "Scouting"—a book that even our War Office should hear of in time. But what future has he besides? We may hope at least that in dignity and reserve it will be worthy of his past.

A Priest of Slums

I N 1902 Father Dolling died, to the relief of
all mediocre, cautious, and half-hearted men
in Church and State. He was too dis-
turbing an element for the official mind that
crawls along the grooves of routine, for the com-
promising mind that seeks the equilibrium of
inactivity, and for the coward who is so solicitous
about the weaker brother. Dolling was a true
soldier-saint, ready to fight any battle provided it
seemed lost, ready to throw over any system provided it seemed dead, and ready to grasp any
weapon that helped to secure the victory of the
soul. The zeal for that victory had eaten him
up. In him we see one of those extremists, those
inspired enthusiasts, who are so rare in all depart-
ments of English life, and naturally rarest among
those who carefully tread the road of the " Via
Media." By Dolling the Via Sacra, the Via
Dolorosa, and the Via Victrix were all known and
loved. But he never could keep straight along the
Via Media, and indeed he never tried. From Irish
air and French ancestry he had absorbed the spirit of
the saint militant here on earth. His eyes were

fixed upon the goal, and not upon the road, and in his passion to arrive we need not wonder that he made rather light of boundaries and notice-boards which to his fellow-travellers seemed not only serviceable but sacred.

It has often been said with sorrow by her most devoted sons that the English Church has no room for saints. It is the fault of the nation rather than the Church, for the English blood runs so little to sainthood that when, about twice in a century, a saint does appear in our midst, we are all a little puzzled to know what to do with him. Bunyan, Fox, the Wesleys, Newman—we need not recall the calendar of sanctity for which the National Church "had no use." Dolling, though he remained in the communion to the last, must be added to the roll. We recognize the difficulties of the Bishops, especially of the present Archbishop of Canterbury, who as Bishop of Winchester brought to an abrupt end Dolling's ten years' battle for righteousness in the worst quarter of Portsmouth. To the officers of the Church, Dolling was very much what Charles Gordon was to the War Office and the Army. Here was something abnormal, an unknown and incalculable quantity. You never could tell where he was going to break out next, he was so painfully unsatisfied with the routine of your level Christian. He reminds us of an adventurous sea-dog boxed in a parlour at Cranford. He spills the tea and rumples the antimacassars. Is it not a kind of old-gentlemanly Cranford, a male spinsterhood, that Canon Scott-Holland describes as one of the greatest dangers to the Church as she is represented in the present Archbishop ?—

"Bishop Davidson's point of danger [he wrote, in the *Commonwealth* for February, 1903] is not the Court. He has survived its perils with a singular simplicity. Rather it is to be sought at the Athenæum. There dwell the sirens who are apt to beguile and bewitch him. They have ceased to be mermaids with harps, and have adopted the disguise of elderly and excellent gentlemen of reputation, who lead you aside into corners, and, in impressive whispers, inform you what will not do, and what the intelligent British public will not stand. Our rulers in the Church may have a deep veneration for the judgment and wisdom of important laity of this type—yet the Athenæum is not the shrine of infallibility. Its elderly common sense has no prophetic afflatus."

But the case was naturally worse for Dolling when he could find little but this elderly common sense pervading the rulers of the Church themselves. In one of his most outspoken criticisms of the Church, written only a year before he died, he says—

"Why cannot the Church get young men from our public schools or universities to answer to the call ? It is because there has been no demand upon their enthusiasm. It has been a nice, easy profession, in which they could live comfortably, settle down and marry, and live very like their brother the squire, although on a poorer scale. . . . Though to-day nearly all the things which the Bishops condemned twenty years ago they recognize and approve, still they have but one opportunist canon of conduct : Be commonplace, be respectable, after the sober manner of the ritual of the Church of England. On the Day of Pentecost it was said of some that they were drunk with new wine. Would to God we could see our prelates thus inebriated ! . . . On no question of any importance, religious or social, have the Bishops given any leading to their people unless they have been driven to it by the man in the street ; and the advice they invariably give is, *Festina lente !*—very wise, indeed, when you occupy the whole position, but fatal when you are leading a forlorn hope."

Dolling was in heart and soul a leader of forlorn hopes. We are willing to admit that he was so good at these exploits as to be comparatively useless for anything else. To call out his highest energies he needed the danger, the excitement, the very hopelessness, perhaps we must say the picturesqueness, of such adventures. Put him in the most depraved and vicious slum on earth, and he became a Happy Warrior. But put him in a respectable suburb ; put him in the monotonous streets of ignoble decency, and he would have withered away from atrophy, from sheer lack of function. Yet we must suppose Dolling himself would have admitted that the ignobly decent and even the suburbs have souls to save. The problem they present to the Churchman is, indeed, far more pressing and more difficult than the question of the thieves, rowdies, and generally vicious persons upon whom the author of Dolling's biography dwells with excessive emphasis. In the East of London the distinctively vicious, the "thieves" and so on, are very few indeed ; they hardly count. Even in Portsmouth they are few in comparison to the regular and hard-working population.

Mr. Osborne, in his "Life of Father Dolling," makes too much of Dolling's remarkable influence over " the very lowest classes." They are the people always easiest to influence, for in them there is always some point of appeal, and at least they are free of self-righteousness and indifferent complacency. That Dolling's power was chiefly displayed in their case is not an evidence of any remarkable strength. If he had converted a respectable suburb, that would have been something for his biographer to brag about ! But of his own special gift—the gift of winning the slums, especially the rowdy slums, by spiritual enthusiasm engrafted on wide human sympathy and personal charm—he certainly made the very utmost that the authorities would allow, and when he speaks of forlorn hopes he is not referring exclusively to attacks upon slum life, but to a continuous assault upon the spiritual inertia of England in general. For such a cause as that he was right in saying that no merely opportunist canon of conduct or doctrine will serve. Man abhors elderly common sense and a dead-level of caution, just as Nature abhors a vacuum, and to the cry of Mediocrity, no matter how Golden, no mortal man ever yet buckled on his armour.

Dolling may, of course, be called a "crank." It is the reward of all pioneers, all enthusiasts, all leaders of thought and action to be called cranks by the dullards whom they puzzle, and the cowards whom they alarm. He refers to the title himself in an address upon America, given at Portsmouth, some two or three years after the Bishop had forced him to resign his mission there by refusing to license the great new church he had built.

"I have always been a 'crank,' and I suppose I always shall be. I suppose, also, I have always been a 'fanatic.' I take it that such persons have their use in any forward movement. A crank is a person who represents a small minority, and who is therefore called a crank by wiser people. . . . I feel that, while cranks are often very disagreeable to the moderate party, still the members of this moderate party often find themselves after a time just where the cranks and fanatics were a few years ago. Then all the moderate people say, 'Well, this is all owing to us; we did it all.' And the cranks and fanatics are perfectly willing that it should be so, and in the end the glory of God is achieved, and the message of the Church proclaimed."

The greatest of torments, at all events, Dolling was spared—he never had doubts. From boyhood up, all through the years at Harrow and Trinity, his beliefs appear to have been always the same. He was not ordained till late, but it was not any religious questionings or hesitation that kept him from his true sphere. For speculation he had neither an interest nor a capacity. He never spent much time in reading, and nearly all his true knowledge was derived from the book of mankind. From the first he plunged into the thick of life, and was only happy amidst its turmoil, its variety, its brilliant colour, its inexhaustible laughter, its passionate distress, and intimate human sympathies. In doctrine he was influenced largely by its visible effect upon the human beings he saw around him. If he saw that prayers for the dead cheered and spiritualized men's souls, he prayed for the dead, and we think that the teaching of the Fathers a thousand years ago or of the sixteenth-century Reformers would have had little weight with him one way or the other against such evidence. As to mere ritual, he always counted that an entirely secondary matter. He was far too zealous a missionary, far too great a humorist, to worry his head about the trivialities of ceremony. As Mr. Osborne writes—

" He tells a story in his ' Ten Years in a Portsmouth Slum ' of his boxing the ears of a Ritualistic youth, who was distressed by his ' incorrectness ' in the mode of holding his hands at the altar. This was characteristic of his attitude towards that Chinese type of religion which revels in ritual correctness of a minute type. Life, Dolling thought, was too short for those discussions about tiny pieces of correctness which fill the correspondence columns of the High Church newspapers."

Dolling was Shakespeare's "bold spirit in a loyal heart." He was anxious to be loyal to the Anglican Church. He remained in her communion, for he saw in her not only the possibilities of spiritual influence, but the remarkable growth of the last seventy years. But then he had the bold spirit—far too bold for "elderly common sense." And so his special powers were continually thwarted; he was removed from his true sphere; for some years in succession he was allowed no sphere at all. It may have been what is called "inevitable;" and yet it is a bad general that does not trust his staff. In many ways Dolling recalls St. Francis—in his humour, his humanity, his love of joy, and his consuming zeal. St. Francis also must have been a difficult person for elderly common sense to deal with; but, as Mr. Osborne notices, Innocent III. knew how to make use of him as the greatest missionary power of his age.

Exuberance

THERE is a generous and high-spirited quality of writing which of late has been rare in our literature. Authors, with all their many virtues of sobriety, lucidity, and truthfulness, have seemed sometimes a little thin and prim. For fifty years they have been rather pale and sad and serious, as though with thinking overmuch, or from too great care for the comfort and salvation of others, and even in their mirth there has remained something shame-faced and self-conscious, as with men who make believe to revel on toast-and-water. Writers on the whole are, we suppose, richer than they were, and we might look for a growing luxuriance and wealth of temperament to correspond with their fortunes. But whether it come of their high living and plain thinking, or whether the cause lie in the monotonous hurry and unsocial crowding of city life, it is certain that literature, in spite of the quantity of books, has been smitten with a kind of a chilliness, a moderation, a caution, a sensitiveness, a depression, a drooping, a melancholy, a squeamishness, a green-sickness, a mediocrity, a wasting, a sterility, and a mope, from which we all suffer.

It is the quality of exuberance that has been lost. There is a kind of writing that swells with fecundity and glows with mirth. It is large and easy and unrestrained. Shake it, and it drops fatness: tap it, and it spouts wine. Of prudence it knows nothing, and it laughs at moderation as Leviathan at the shaking of a spear. It loves the gifts of the sunburnt old earth, and counts them over again and again like a child counting his birthday toys. Its voice is deep and mellow, with a laugh far down in the throat. It grows, like a gourd, with sitting in the sun, and it loves best the plentiful lands of vine and olive, calm rivers and grey poplar trees. Yet once it has been found in all its lavish abundance even under our own distempered sky; for only three men in the world's history have possessed exuberance in full perfection, and one of them was Falstaff. The other two were Aristophanes and Rabelais. But there are a certain few besides whose fortune it has been to be born with some gill, runlet, tierce, puncheon, hogshead, bucketful, or butt of it in their blood, which is ever merrily asserting itself, like the "dash of the tar-brush" visible in lamb's-wool hair and the gulf of a laughing mouth.

Such certainly was Dumas, who had it almost in brimming measure, as might be seen from his loose shoulders and rolling chest; such was Cyrano, as was evident from the promontory of his nose. Such

might Victor Hugo have been, had he not turned
portentous ; and Whitman, had he but laughed ;
and Swift, had he not dwelt, as Coleridge said,
"in a dry place ; " and Jean Paul, had he not
dwelt in Germany. But from England we may
admit Fielding into the overflowing fellowship, and
Smollett, and Sterne, and Boz, and Byron when he
is not giving himself airs. And we would gladly
take in Meredith, did he not think such a plaguey
lot. A few more still might be counted, but many
would claim entrance against whom the tavern door
must be shut ; for though there is no black-list in
the realm of Abundantia, the corruption of exuberance is vulgarity—a thing most plentiful, but no
more truly related than a Cockney pair-oared boat
hired by three men bound for Eel-pie Island is
related to the bulging galleon which, stuffed with
Spanish merchandize, is borne by saffron sails from
Cadiz to the Brazils.

Among present writers Mr. Hilaire Belloc has
something of this opulence and unexhausted spirit.
Perhaps it comes from some fag-end of a French
sunbeam that has survived a transportation ; though
we must avoid the mistake he mentions of a crowd
that took a fellow-citizen for a Frenchman, and
treated him accordingly because he had blacked his
face like a negro. By whatever origin, he possesses
the bubbling copiousness, the fertile resource, the
rubicund speech, the passion for words, the hatred

of facts, the glorious lying, the cheery assault, the honest irreverence, the carelessness, thriftlessness, and abandonment that recall the three great ensamples of exuberance. His " Path to Rome " was littered with such plenty, and now again it overflows in a new production, with double titles, like giant twins : " The Aftermath ; or, Gleanings from a Busy Life," called upon the outer cover for purposes of sale, " Caliban's Guide to Letters," and to be bought of Messrs. Duckworth for eighteen-pence, two shillings, or as much more as an exuberant purchaser may be pleased to fling over the counter with the cry, " Mais quel geste ! "

In it we see what Carlyle's German Professor identified with " Satan's Invisible World Revealed : " we see the journalist's progress from his review to his pulping-room. And the journalist is conducted along that road by as fine a guardian-angel as ever discovered the voice of one whimpering in a cabbage garden, or made the fortune of tender mediocrity. Dr. Caliban (indifferently, on successive pages, spoken of as James and Thomas) is a noble embodiment of the commonplace upon which common sense is so securely founded as a home for the lords of the world and the top-hatted race. As quite a youth he had been a strenuous opponent of American slavery ; " he might have been called the most prominent Abolitionist in Worcestershire, and worked indefatigably for the cause in so far as it concerned this country." A similar passion for freedom and justice inspired his later life—

" Russia he hated as the oppressor of Finland and Poland, for oppression he loathed and combatted wherever it appeared ; nor had Mr. Arthur Balfour a stronger supporter than he when that statesman, armed only in the simple manliness of an English Christian and Freeman, combatted and destroyed the terrorism that stalked through Ireland."

So also, in his great speech at St. James's Hall upon the Dreyfus case, standing for truth and justice, he began his peroration with the courageous words : " England will yet weather the storm." Yet at fitting times his tact was a serviceable ally to his courage, for we read : " A young radical of sorts was declaiming at his table one evening against the concentration camps. Dr. Caliban listened patiently, and at the end of the harangue said gently, ' Shall we join the ladies ? ' The rebuke was not lost."

It is lamentable to hear that so worthy a representative of average intelligence is now confined in an establishment for the mentally afflicted, but we may hope that, like the epileptic mentioned in another part of the book, he may be restored to a normal, and even commonplace, state of mind. We proceed at once to the practical lessons which the author derived from Dr. Caliban's principles and example, such as the complete art of reviewing, illustrated by a series of suitable notices upon the following subject :—

"The book was called, 'The Snail : Its Habitat, Food, Customs, Virtues, Vices, and Future.' It was, as its title would imply, a monograph upon snails, and there were many fine coloured prints, showing various snails occupied in feeding on the leaves proper to each species. It also contained a large number of process blocks, showing sections, plans, elevations, and portraits of snails, as well as detailed descriptions (with diagrams) of the ears, tongues, eyes, hair, and nerves of snails. It was a comprehensive and remarkable work."

The reviewer composed his notices (eight or ten in all) in accordance with the varying information he received from his editor as to the political opinions of the author and the publisher's willingness to advertise. We can heartily recommend them as models to all dustmen, literary scavengers, beginners and past-masters in reviewing, chiffoniers, rag-and-bone men, and ghouls ; just as we can recommend all the chapters of advice that follow, upon Political Appeals, Short Stories, Short Lyrics, Interviews, Personal Pars, Editing, Revelations, and Special Prose. Two extravaganzas, monstrosities, or tales, are shot in, besides an Index to the Pulping Room, one of them, on the shrine of St. Loup, opening with the true Aristophanic-Rabelaisian revelry in strings and masses of words—

"My excellent good Dreyfusards, anti-Dreyfusards, Baptists, Anabaptists, Premonstratensians, antiquaries, sterling fellows, foreign correspondents, home readers, historians, Nestorians, philosophers, Deductionists, Inductionists,

Prætorians (I forgot them), Cæsarists, Lazarists, Catholics, Protestants, Agnostics and militant Atheists, as also all you Churchmen, Nonconformists, Particularists, very strong Secularists, and even you, my well-beloved little brethren called the Peculiar People, give ear attentively and listen to what is to follow, and you shall learn more of a matter that has woefully disturbed you than ever you would get from the *Daily Mail* or from Mynheer Van Damm, or even from Dr. Biggles's ' Walks and Talks in France.' "

The other extravaganza, monstrosity, or tale, is the diverting and instructive short story how Mr. Thorpe, drysalter, fell into the river near Cleopatra's Needle (the incident of a short story " should take place on the sea or in brackish, or at least tidal, waters ")—fell into the river and was immediately hooked out, and how this epic incident (" Mr. Davidson's shorter lyrics have no better claim to be epic in their essentials than has this relation of ' The Accident to Mr. Thorpe ' ")—how this epic incident grew in Mr. Thorpe's mind till he told the adventure at large to every man in the street, steamboat, railway carriage, omnibus, waiting-room, bar, church porch, or chapel door, with superb amplifications of detail—" sometimes it was in the ' steep water off the Banks ; ' sometimes in ' the glassy steaming seas and on the feverish coast of the Bight ; ' sometimes it was ' a point or two norr'ard of the Owers light,' but it was always terrible, graphic, and a lie "— and finally he left all his considerable fortune to the Lifeboat Fund, which badly needed it. All such appeals to history, scientific diversions, facts, false-hoods, and foundations for theories—together with the pleasant ode on Mr. Chamberlain's return and the interview with the patriotic poet who showed no jealousy at the hallucination of a red-hot brass monkey attempting song—all such satires, ironies, and overflows of milk and honey, we must now leave to the plumpy and well-conditioned hearts that love to drink the wine of exuberance in whatever ocean, river, mill-stream, gutter, or down-spout it may run.

The Faith of Literature

A RECENT article in a literary journal ended with this quotation from Herbert Spencer : " Of the ends to be kept in view by the legislator, all are unimportant compared to the end of character-making. This alone is national education." We repeat the sentence, not so much for the truth it contains, as simply because it was quoted. Here are words which, in practice, nobody believes. Legislators do not believe them, for when they talk of the necessity of improving our education they always point to the danger of commercial rivalry. When they tell us we ought to study modern languages, do they mean that modern languages form character ? Not a bit of it. They mean that modern languages produce good bagmen. When Lord Rosebery urges us to spend any amount of money on a Technical Institute like the Charlottenburg Polytechnic, does he argue that technical institutes conduce to character-making ? Not at all. His real argument is that, unless we improve in chemistry, the Germans will continue to undersell us in chemical dyes and chemical wines. But our legislators are not to blame, for it is the same with parents. Nearly all of them choose a public school where the richest people send their sons, provided it is just within their own means ; the remainder choose the school most like to train a boy best for his future profession, whether technical or learned. It never occurs to them that all these things—acquaintance with the nobility and the rich, skill in handicraft, knowledge of the classics, or fame in cricket—are unimportant compared with the end of character-making. In all probability it has never occurred to them that education has anything to do with character at all.

And yet Herbert Spencer was right. When the truth is stated, most people would now admit it, though no one acts upon it yet. It is a truth on the way to recognition. It was proclaimed in the faith that some day it would be recognized, and there can be no doubt the faith will be justified. That it has been stated some thirty or forty years and is not yet realized makes no difference to its truth, and faith can always afford to wait. Waiting is its trade.

Or take another instance of a very similar kind. William Blake said, "The wretched state of the arts originates in the wretched state of political science (which is the science of sciences)." The saying is true in the main, though to Blake's contemporaries it must have appeared only another evidence of his insanity. Since his day Ruskin has come and proclaimed the same doctrine for sixty years without ceasing. Most people are now aware that the doctrine has a glimmering of sense, and very many would admit its truth. But in practice it is still almost universally believed that the arts can be improved by the multiplication of art schools, and that the increased number of paintings which rich people hang upon their walls is an evidence of the improvement. In actual life it is never realized that " the wretched state of the arts " originates in the "wretched state of political science." Even if we grant that the condition of the arts has improved since Blake's day, the general idea of his doctrine is still waiting for recognition. But that it has to wait— that even Ruskin's sweet voice, captivating all hearers for so many years, has not brought its realization much nearer—this does not in the least affect its truth. In those periods when the daily lives of a people are hideous and degraded, the arts take tone from their surrounding. Whether the people and their governors recognize this or not, makes no difference at all. It is a matter of faith ; it may be recognized in time.

And what is seen to be true in the practical doctrines of education and political science, is even more obviously true in literature. All good literature must be written in faith. That is its necessary condition. The writer's appeal is not immediate like an actor's or an orator's, or even like a painter's, a sculptor's, or a musician's. Its form is invisible, and in modern times usually inaudible too. It works solely upon the lonely mind, and has no outward aid. Nor can its effect be tested by anything like the demonstrations of a theatre. A novelist once saw a young person blush over one of his books. An Emperor once saw a dull person laughing over Don Quixote. But such visible expressions of emotion are rare, and in these days of print, the author himself can hardly ever hope to witness them. That is why he of all working people needs most faith. He has to cast his bread upon the waters, but it is extremely unlikely that he will find it again after many days. And (without driving a metaphor too far) we may say that the better the bread, the less chance he has of finding it.

Instances are almost too obvious, but let us take the highest of all, and remember that it was only by a mere fluke that Shakespeare's best plays were even thought worth preserving. Or, to take the case of Blake again, what chance of recognition had the "Songs of Innocence" in 1789? Within some thirty or forty years Charles Lamb and Wordsworth had discovered them. Within another fifty or sixty years after that they became the common property of all who love literature ; but by what faith in beauty and in man's ultimate recognition of beauty must the poet have been inspired, who at the time when English verse had perhaps touched its lowest point could raise the song of " The Echoing Green," or "The Chimney-Sweeper," or "The Divine Image," or that song of " Night," with its metre of subtle and varying beauty. For a hundred and fifty years nothing to compare with such things had been heard in England, and the world around Blake was contemptuously deaf to them. He could only write in faith that some day human beings would again be born with minds sufficiently like his own to perceive the beauty of his work. To remove a mountain is a trivial task compared with the confidence of so vast a change ; and yet the change came.

It is this faith in the ultimate similarity of great minds which makes great literature possible, for not even genius could produce without the hope that at some time its work would be taken at its value. An evidence for the faith may be seen in the peculiarity of all the work of the highest genius—that it appears capable of growth, no matter how old it has become. There are passages in Homer and Shakespeare which it has been impossible for the world to appreciate or understand till this very moment. They appear to have been growing with the world, so much more can the world discover in them now than at any past time. This is why the works and teachings of the highest genius are rightly called immortal. They never grow old because they are always growing new. Any one with five years' courage may test this quality of excellence for himself. Let him take some great book, like the Bible, which has been familiar

to him from his childhood.   Let him seal it up for
five years and try to forget all about it while he
goes on leading an active life, travels, associates
with various kinds of men, works hard, and reads
occasionally.   Then let him open the sealed book
again, and he will find what a different thing it has
become whilst it has lain apparently so still.   Much
of it may have rotted away and become abhorrent,
but the best part, the part of genius, will have gained
a lustre, a kindling depth of meaning, of which he
had no conception before.   With what a sweet shock
of revelation will the man who has lived in mining
circles, or in clubs and Courts, or among philanthropists, come upon that passage about considering
the lilies !   It was trite with the tramplings of ten
thousand clergy, but now it has recovered and
grown ; it sparkles with new rays like the frost ; it
is seen to include the garment of the soul as well as
of the body ; it is the secret of genius ; it is the law
of life.

"I was not in safety, neither had I rest, neither
was I quiet ; yet trouble came."   When the poet of
Job wrote that astonishing paradox, he was feeling
out to an age still hidden by four thousand years
from his own.   It sometimes seems as though no
one could have understood his meaning till the
days of Carlyle.   What did mankind realize of
Montaigne's friendship for Steven de la Boitie till
Walter Pater came ?   Or who has sailed with Drake

and Hawkins till to-day? These are but diverse instances of the power of faith by which men, who have grasped at the very heart of life, have put on record the thing they found in assured confidence that the human mind at its moments of greatness is always the same, and that the highest human thought possesses in itself the growing power of immortality. Those who work for the moment have their reward. In every generation they have audience fit though many. Plenty of the mediocre, the indifferent, the good-enough can always be had to meet the passing demand. That is why the mediocre, the indifferent, the good-enough can never survive, for next year's season snows them over with a fall of the same quality, and they are at rest. "What recks it them? What need they? They are sped." But the few who have ears to listen to the voice of life herself, must work by faith. They speak to their kindred in far-off places and far-off times, assured of recognition, for, as the poet said, the gods are known to each other.

THE END